19 famous gay and lesbian relationships, the age of each partner when they first met, and how long each relationship lasted • 8 memorable gay love offerings • Ages when 12 famous men first had sex with another man • 14 men who loved boys • 24 famous people who acknowledged having had at least one homosexual experience in their lives • 15 famous men who have publicly denied being gay • 18 famous people who had gay or bisexual sons • 7 famous gay men who also had a gay brother • 7 supposed references to homosexuality in the Bible • The 11 U.S. metropolitan areas with the most gay bars, and the approximate number in
each • 21 maj … : common ex-
planations for … s of homosexuality • 11 al … ic terms for a
gay man • 8 a … origins for the
word "faggot" … iked the word
gay • 19 class … ay movement
doesn't want … l about • Or-
dinary people … hoaxes • 20
famous gay o … s • 35 major
companies th … st Potter's 10
characteristics … er's 7 ways to
spot homosex … 10 men who
were paid at l … for gay sex •
13 sex practic … ways to have
fun in bed • 4 … reputed to be
aphrodisiacs • … performance
• 12 famous p … popular posi-
tions for jacki … • 9 Victorian
"cures" for ma … asturbation •
Hung like a horse: Average erect penis lengths for 10 species • 16 famous men, all reputedly very well hung • 6 famous male nudes • 15 eighteenth-century slang expressions for cock • 20 nineteenth-century slang expressions for cock • The origins of 7 common sex-related words • 10 words or phrases that sound obscene, but aren't • 12 provocatively named businesses • 17 famous people who had syphilis • 4 men it would have been better not to go home with • 20 male sex symbols and how old each was in 1988 • 8 heartthrobs from the past and how old each would be if he were alive in 1988 • 12 examples of gays on network television • 5 prominent actors who turned down the role of Zach, the doctor, in "Making Love" • 5 movies that in some way deal with homosexuality, and what the mainstream critics said about each • 43 notable actors who have appeared in drag in the movies • 36 hot actors who shucked their clothes for the cameras, and in what movies you can see them naked • 9 on-screen mouth-to-mouth kisses between men • From Sappho to *The Joy of Gay Sex:* 15 outrageous acts of censorship in the history of gay people • 19 books recently banned, or nearly banned, because of gay or lesbian themes • 3 suppressed manuscripts of famous gay men • 5 "dirty" gay novels written before 1930 • 2 unfinished gay novels by famous writers • 12 countries and when each decriminalized homosexual acts between consenting adults • 22 countries in which homosexuality is still specifically proscribed by la … tured or ex-
ecuted gay m … nting adults
are still a crime • The 5 states with the harshest criminal penalties for homosexual sodomy • 24 famous men who were arrested on gay sex or morals charges •

THE GAY BOOK OF LISTS

Leigh W. Rutledge

Boston • Alyson Publications

Typeset and printed in the United States of America.

Portraits of Horatio Alger, John Harvey Kellogg, Stephen Crane, Emma Goldman, Henry James, Walt Whitman, and George Santayana reproduced from the *Dictionary of American Portraits*, published by Dover Publications, Inc., 1967.

Published as a trade paperback original by Alyson Publications, Inc., 40 Plympton Street, Boston, Mass. 02118.
Distributed in England by GMP Publishers, P.O. Box 247, London N17 9QR England.

First edition, first printing: November 1987
Second printing: July 1988
Third printing: August 1989
Fourth printing: February 1992

ISBN 1-55583-120-6

CONTENTS

To RICHARD, and
to the memory of
DR. ALLAN SIMMONS

FOREWORD AND ACKNOWLEDGEMENTS

"If you ever start a homo household," my mother once told me in a rare moment of asperity, "don't ever expect me to set foot in it." She and my father had found out from my sister that I was gay. My father took the news of my sexuality in a self-congratulating "I always suspected" sort of way. He had always preferred my older brother, and this latest information about me further justified that preference in his mind. "I accept it, but don't evei expect me to approve of it," he said. My mother, on the other hand, was devastated: she contemplated seeing a lawyer to disown me; she taped newspaper articles on hepatitis and rectal cancer to the dashboard of my car (thank God, this was before all of the publicity about AIDS, or the inside of my car would have looked like a supermarket bulletin board); and it was suddenly obvious to her that I had all along been a product of my *father's* side of the family. I was an imposter. She was hurt and confused, and even now, more than ten years later, they both have a difficult time surmounting their deep sense of propriety about these things.

Now you may ask, legitimately: what the hell does any of this have to do with *The Gay Book of Lists*? Actually — everything. The muddle with my parents — and the ever more apparent muddle of the world around me, especially in regard to sexual matters — set me on a search for identity that ended, perhaps predictably, with my owning a 20' by 4' walk-in closet lined with file cabinets and bookcases full of clippings, articles, and whole publications — both rare and common — full of almost everything I could ever get my hands on about homosexuality, gayness, gay life, gay men. It's said that a man who hoards gold must have a heart of stone; so what then can be said about the heart of a man who hoards trivia and history's gossip, all of it centering around the subject of his sexuality? He's been looking for himself, that's for sure. Haven't we all?

This compulsion combines quite nicely with some of my nervous habits. Some people doodle; some pace; others talk to themselves; I do all three, *and* I write lists. Maybe it's only a way of trying to create order out of an exasperating universe, or a way of trying to justify to myself all of the compulsive collecting I've done. More likely, it is simply a form of entertainment and a delightful way of blowing off steam.

A word of caution: the majority of these lists are not meant to be comprehensive. When I write about "17 Outspoken Anti-Gay Politicians" or "8 Memorable Gay Love Offerings" or "4 Men It Would Have Been Better Not to Go Home With," I'm aware that any one of them could be expanded and that, in the case of a list like "9 Perfectly Disgusting Reactions to AIDS," the entries could conceivably go on and on. What I have included reflects my own interests and prejudices. Also, it seems necessary to point out that although there is some material on lesbians and lesbianism in this book, the overwhelming focus is on gay men, and I must leave it to someone else more qualified to one day write a definitive *Lesbian Book of Lists.*

For their help in providing me with information or assistance, I would like to take a moment to thank: Bill Baumer, the Centers for Disease Control in Atlanta, Richard Donley, the late Dr. William Halberstadt, Sue Hyde at the National Gay and Lesbian Task Force, John Phelps, Edna F. Riley, Libby Rutledge, Chris Schick, the late Dr. Allan Simmons, Charlotte Simmons, Peter Urbanek, Dennis Waite, the office of Congressman Ted Weiss, and my publisher, Sasha Alyson. In particular, I owe an enormous debt to Sam Staggs; without his constant help and advice, this book probably would never have seen the light of day. However, any errors that may have crept into this work are solely my responsibility.

Finally, I would enjoy hearing from anyone who has comments, additions, corrections, questions, or even complaints about *The Gay Book of Lists.* Those so inclined should write to:

Leigh W. Rutledge
P.O. Box 5523
Pueblo, Colorado 81002

THE GAY BOOK OF LISTS

19 FAMOUS GAY AND LESBIAN RELATIONSHIPS, THE AGE OF EACH PARTNER WHEN THEY FIRST MET, AND HOW LONG EACH RELATIONSHIP LASTED

1. ROMAINE BROOKS (41) and
   NATALIE BARNEY (39): 53 years
2. PETER PEARS (26) and
   BENJAMIN BRITTEN (23): 40 years
3. GERTRUDE STEIN (33) and
   ALICE B. TOKLAS (30): 39 years
4. W.H. AUDEN (32) and
   CHESTER KALLMAN (18): 34 years
5. CHRISTOPHER ISHERWOOD (48) and
   DON BACHARDY (18): 32 years
6. EDWARD CARPENTER (54) and
   GEORGE MERRILL (26): 30 years
7. W. SOMERSET MAUGHAM (40) and
   GERALD HAXTON (22): 29 years
8. SYLVIA BEACH (30) and
   ADRIENNE MONNIER (25): 20 years
9. W. SOMERSET MAUGHAM (72) and
   ALAN SEARLE (41): 19 years
10. KENNETH HALLIWELL (25) and
    JOE ORTON (18): 16 years
11. PIERS GAVESTON (16) and
    EDWARD II (14): 14 years
12. TENNESSEE WILLIAMS (36) and
    FRANKIE MERLO (22): 14 years
13. OSCAR WILDE (37) and
    LORD ALFRED DOUGLAS (21): 9 years
14. WALT WHITMAN (46) and
    PETER DOYLE (18): 8 years
15. HADRIAN (48) and
    ANTINOUS (15): 6 years

16. JEAN COCTEAU (30) and RAYMOND RADIGUET (16): 4 years
17. SERGE DIAGHILEV (37) and VASLAV NIJINSKY (19): 4 years
18. ROCK HUDSON (57) and MARC CHRISTIAN (29): 4 years
19. PAUL VERLAINE (27) and ARTHUR RIMBAUD (17): 2 years

8 MEMORABLE GAY LOVE OFFERINGS

1. *CHRISTOPHER AND HIS KIND* AND *DOWN THERE ON A VISIT*

Writer Christopher Isherwood dedicated several of his books — including *Christopher and His Kind* and *Down There on a Visit* — to his lover of over thirty years, artist Don Bachardy. Bachardy, in turn, often provided affectionate drawings of Isherwood for the books' covers.

2. SOME OPERAS

English composer Benjamin Britten wrote all of his major tenor roles, and most of his solo vocal works, specifically for his lover, tenor Peter Pears. The operas include *Peter Grimes, A Midsummer Night's Dream, Billy Budd,* and *Death in Venice* — the greatest English operas since Purcell.

3. *THE COUNTERFEITERS*

In 1916, Andre Gide began work on his only novel, *The Counterfeiters,* in order to woo and impress sixteen-year-old Marc Allegret, with whom Gide, then forty-seven, had fallen in love. Allegret was apparently suitably charmed: the two enjoyed a long, intimate relationship. Allegret later became a well-known film director.

4. INDEPENDENCE FOR ARABIA

British soldier and adventurer T.E. Lawrence dedicated his masterpiece, *The Seven Pillars of Wisdom,* "To S.A." — Salim

Ahmed, a handsome Arab boy he had loved. Ahmed had died a few years before the book's publication. A love poem accompanied Lawrence's dedication. Lawrence also claimed that the motivation during his entire campaign to drive the Turks from Arabia had been "personal." "I liked a particular Arab," he said, referring to Ahmed, "and I thought that freedom for the race would be an acceptable present."

5. THE *PATHETIQUE* SYMPHONY

Tchaikovksy's Sixth Symphony, the *Pathetique,* was dedicated to his nephew, Vladimir Davidov, with whom the composer was deeply in love. Tchaikovsky wrote of the symphony, "I love it as I have never loved a single one of my offspring."

6. ROYAL PATRONAGE

After falling in love with composer Richard Wagner, King Ludwig II, the eighteen-year-old monarch of Bavaria, paid off Wagner's enormous debts, provided him with housing and an income, and arranged for extravagant productions of Wagner's operas in Munich — all in an attempt to keep the composer near him. Even after the two broke off their intimacy, Ludwig continued to provide Wagner with homes, financial support, and the critical funds needed to finish the opera house at Bayreuth, which Wagner was building in the 1870s.

7. AN INSCRIPTION

When archaeologists excavated the ruins of Pompeii and Herculaneum, they discovered a profusion of ancient graffiti, much of it erotic, scribbled on various walls throughout the cities. One such inscription records the relationship enjoyed by two men, and reads simply: "Auctus fucked Quintius here." We know nothing about either Auctus or Quintius, except for the pleasure they shared two thousand years ago.

8. THE MOST SPECTACULAR FUNERAL IN HISTORY

Alexander the Great had the body of his dead lover, Hephaestion, burned atop an awesome 200-foot pyre, erected at a cost of over 10,000 talents, equivalent to roughly $60 million today. The pyre, which took months to complete, contained tiers of sculpted ships, centaurs, bulls, sirens, lions, and wreaths, all in combustible softwood. Plans were made for an even more spectacular lasting memorial: the carving of Mount Athos, the *entire* mountain, into a huge likeness of Hephaestion, so large that a small town of 10,000 people could fit in the palm of the statue's left hand. However, work on the project was never begun, and Alexander himself died less than a year after Hephaestion.

AGES WHEN 12 FAMOUS MEN FIRST HAD SEX WITH ANOTHER MAN

1. KRISTEN BJORN (b. 1957), Swedish model and photographer

When he was seventeen, he met and lost his virginity to an eighteen-year-old French Canadian boy in Lisbon. "We spent a month together making love on the windy beaches at night before it was time to go our separate ways," Bjorn said later. "I was heartbroken when it was time to part."

2. CONSTANTINE CAVAFY (1863-1933), Greek poet

Cavafy had sex for the first time with another man in 1883, when he was twenty years old and living in Constantinople. His first partner was apparently one of his cousins.

3. CHRISTOPHER ISHERWOOD (1904-1986), English-U.S. writer

He realized he was gay when he was ten, and often had orgasms wrestling with other boys. He was also sexually attracted to his father. "I used to go into his dressing room in the morning while he was doing physical exercises almost naked, in his undershorts," he once said. "I can still remember liking the hardness of his muscles and the smell of his body." But it wasn't until Isherwood was in college, and was in his late teens or early twenties, that he actually first had sex with another man.

4. DAVID KOPAY (b. 1942), U.S. football pro

He was twenty or twenty-one when he first had sex with an other man. His partner was a fraternity brother at the University of Washington. The two of them had been out one night drinking beer. When they came home, they collapsed in bed together. "We kept our clothes on," Kopay wrote in his autobiography, "but I had an orgasm just from rubbing against Ted and holding him." They repeated the experience numerous times while they were in college together, eventually having intercourse and oral sex.

5. ANDRE GIDE (1869-1951), French writer

Gide was twenty-three when he lost his virginity to a fourteen-year-old Arab boy named Ali in Tunisia. The two had sex in the sand dunes.

6. TENNESSEE WILLIAMS (1912-1983), U.S. playwright

Although he'd had wet dreams and spontaneous orgasms, he didn't even masturbate until he was twenty-seven, and it wasn't until he was twenty-eight that he first had sex with another man — a paratrooper in New Orleans.

7. JOHN ADDINGTON SYMONDS (1840-1893), English essayist and historian

Symonds anguished over his homosexual impulses for years, and suffered from one physical malady after another as he tried to suppress them. At the age of thirty-six, he finally hired "a brawny young soldier" to have sex with him at a male brothel in London. The experience, Symonds wrote, "exercised a powerful effect upon my life." It did not cure his physical maladies — in fact, he suffered a severe relapse of lung disease shortly afterward — but it set him on the road to coming to grips with his real nature.

8. FRED HALSTED (b. 1941), U.S. porno star

He was eight years old when he was forced to have sex with his stepfather. "At that age, I didn't know what rape was," he said later. "I didn't know what had happened to me. I wasn't repulsed, but I couldn't accept it . . . My interest in sadism, my fascination, had its roots in that early incident."

9. E.M. FORSTER (1879-1970), English writer

Forster spent his teens and twenties in a state of unrelieved sexual frustration. Finally, when he was thirty-one, a long-time friend made love to him on a sitting-room sofa; it was the first time Forster had any kind of physical encounter with another man. "After so long a delay," biographer P.N. Furbank wrote, "the event was not, after all, of much significance to Forster."

10. OSCAR WILDE (1854-1900), British playwright and wit
Wilde was thirty-two — and had already been married for two years — before he actually had sex with another man.

11. LEONARD MATLOVICH (b. 1943), gay rights activist and former Air Force sergeant
He became famous in 1975, and appeared on the cover of *Time* magazine, when he set himself up as a test case to challenge the U.S. military's policy of automatically discharging homosexuals. Although he knew he was gay at the age of twelve, he was celibate until he was thirty, when he finally got up the nerve to go to a gay bar in Pensacola, Florida. He lost his virginity to a government civil servant.

12. W. SOMERSET MAUGHAM (1874-1965), British writer
Maugham was sixteen and studying in Heidelberg, Germany when he first had sex with another man, a 26-year-old British student he met there.

14 MEN WHO LOVED BOYS

1. EPISTHENES (4th century B.C.), Greek soldier
He tried to intervene in the public execution of a remarkably handsome teenage boy he had never seen before. Totally captivated by the youth's looks and anguished at the thought of such beauty being destroyed, Episthenes begged the executioner to stop and offered his own life in place of the boy's. After some discussion, in which friends testified to Episthenes' bravery in battle and his passion for beautiful boys, the handsome youth was spared, and Episthenes walked off with him.

2. DEMETRIUS I (336-283 B.C.), Macedonian king
He was so enamored of a beautiful Greek youth named Damocles that he followed the teenager everywhere, hoping to seduce him. The boy, however, was known not only for his beauty but for his virtue as well, and he fled in horror from the king's relentless sexual advances. Finally, tracked down and cornered in a public bathhouse by the king, Damocles quickly

searched for a means of escape. Finding none, he jumped into a cauldron of boiling water rather than compromise himself – a suicide that Plutarch later called "untimely and unmerited, but worthy of the beauty that occasioned it."

3. CATULLUS (84-54 B.C.), Roman poet

In his poems, he liked to boast of his conquests of teenage boys, and bragged that once, after surprising a boy and girl in the act of making love, he mounted the boy "to please Venus." Disappointed in love by the beautiful nymphomaniac Clodia, he turned to an equally beautiful boy, Juventius. However, Juventius was fickle and cruel, and the affair was stormy, to say the least. Catullus, who was barely thirty when he died, expressed disgust for most homosexuals, except those who were active lovers of boys.

4. NERO (A.D. 37-68), Roman emperor

He tried to turn one of his slave-boys, Sporus, into a girl by castration, then went through a public wedding ceremony with him – dowry, bridal veil, and all. A popular joke at the time was that the world would have been a happier place had Nero's father, Domitius, married that sort of wife.

5. STRATO (2nd century), Greek poet

One of the most cheerfully gluttonous boy chasers of the ancient world, Strato was the editor and primary author of the *Musa Puerilis,* an anthology of over two hundred epigrams devoted to the subject of boy-love. He blithely confessed, in one poem, that "I like a boy's body when he's hot from the park, and his flesh glistens with oil. I like a boy with grime on his body, not with the pretty enchantment of the romantics."

6. LEONARDO DA VINCI (1452-1519), Italian artist and inventor

At the age of 38, Leonardo "adopted" a beautiful but roguish ten-year-old boy, nicknamed Salai, "Little Devil." His presence in Leonardo's home has perplexed scholars for centuries, since Salai was neither exactly a servant nor an apprentice, and since Leonardo himself described the boy (always with a certain exasperated affection) as a "thieving, lying, obstinate" glutton. In his journals, Leonardo kept an exact running tally of everything the boy stole: money from friends, money from Leonardo's wallet, boots, silver. The boy grew into a handsome and charming young

U.S. novelist Horatio Alger. Among his works was the boys' book *Ragged Dick, or Street Life in New York.* Alger used the revenues from his books to help finance orphanages and homes for runaway boys.

man; but still a thief and a liar. He had a taste for beautiful clothes, especially shoes. According to one of Leonardo's biographers, Salai owned "quite a fantastic number of pairs of shoes." Leonardo and the boy remained inseparable companions for nearly twenty-six years.

7. MICHELANGELO (1475-1564), Italian sculptor and painter

Michelangelo was in his late sixties when he met Cecchino dei Bracci, the charming and beautiful fifteen-year-old nephew of one of his friends. Of the boy's beauty, he wrote: "With his face God wished to correct nature." When Bracci died in 1544, at the age of sixteen, Michelangelo designed the boy's tomb and wrote no fewer than fifty poems mourning his passing. Other boys thought to have been Michelangelo's lovers were: Gherardo Perini, a muscular, strikingly beautiful young male model whose relationship with Michelangelo was the subject of much gossip at the time; Tommaso Cavalieri, an intelligent and handsome young nobleman who remained one of Michelangelo's lifelong friends; and Febo di Poggio, a young male prostitute of whom Michelangelo wrote, "Up from the earth I rose with his wings, and death itself I could have found sweet."

8. CHRISTOPHER MARLOWE (1564-1593), English dramatist

Marlowe's tastes were best characterized by his famous epigram, "All they that love not tobacco and boys are fools."

9. HORATIO ALGER (1834-1899), U.S. novelist

As pastor of the Unitarian Church in Brewster, Massachusetts, he befriended many of the local boys, and took them on seaside picnics. Two of the boys eventually stepped forward and confessed they had engaged in homosexual acts with the 34-year-old Alger. Confronted, Alger did not deny it. He was run out of town, and fled to New York City, where he achieved national fame writing stories for boys. He later became a tireless philanthropist working to improve conditions for homeless youths, orphans, and runaways.

10. OSCAR WILDE (1854-1900), Irish dramatist and wit

Wilde claimed to prefer lower-class boys because "their passion was all body and no soul." He once bragged to a friend of having made love to five different boys in a single night. "I kissed each one of them in every part of their bodies," he said. "They were all dirty and appealed to me just for that reason."

11. FRIEDRICH ALFRED KRUPP (1854-1902), German industrialist

The multimillionaire German industrialist set up a lavish private pleasure palace in a grotto on Capri, where he entertained under-age Italian boys, mostly the sons of local fishermen. Sex was performed to the accompaniment of a live string quartet, and orgasms were celebrated with bursts of fireworks. When Krupp's wife, back home in Germany, heard rumors of what was going on, she went straight to the Kaiser — who promptly had her committed to an insane asylum. The Krupp industrialist empire was too vital to German national security to be compromised by such stories, even if true. However, the German press eventually found out about Krupp's private orgies, and printed the whole story, complete with damning photographs taken by Krupp himself inside the grotto. Rather than face disgrace, Krupp committed suicide.

12. CONSTANTINE CAVAFY (1863-1933), Greek poet

Living in Alexandria, Egypt, he frequented houses of prostitution where strong, well-built Greek boys (most of them poor and with wretched jobs during the day) earned extra money having sex with older men. He bribed his servants to ruffle up his bedsheets so that his mother wouldn't suspect he had been out all night.

13. ANDRE GIDE (1869-1951), French writer

Having lost his virginity, at the age of twenty-three, to a fourteen-year-old Arab youth in Tunisia, he later fell in love with a fifteen-year-old servant boy in Algeria. Gide longed to take the boy back with him to France, but Gide's mother opposed the idea: she couldn't stand the idea of a "Negro," as she called him, living with them in Paris. When he was forty-seven, Gide fell in love and had an affair with sixteen-year-old Marc Allegret.

14. WILLIAM S. BURROUGHS (b. 1914), U.S. writer

Laid up in a hospital in Tangier, he used to fantasize about the boys at an Italian school across the street and often watched them with his binoculars. On another occasion, he and a friend paid two Arab boys sixty cents to have sex in front of them. "We demanded semen too," Burroughs later wrote, "no half-assed screwing." Burroughs has said that "homosexuality is a worldwide economic fact. In poor countries — like Morocco and parts of Italy — it's one of the big industries, one of the main ways in which a young boy can get somewhere."

24 FAMOUS PEOPLE WHO ACKNOWLEDGED HAVING HAD AT LEAST ONE HOMOSEXUAL EXPERIENCE IN THEIR LIVES

1. VOLTAIRE (1694-1778), French philosopher
2. GIOVANNI GIACOMO CASANOVA (1725-1798), Italian adventurer and libertine
3. WINSTON CHURCHILL (1875-1961), British prime minister
4. CARL JUNG (1875-1961), Swiss founder of analytical psychology

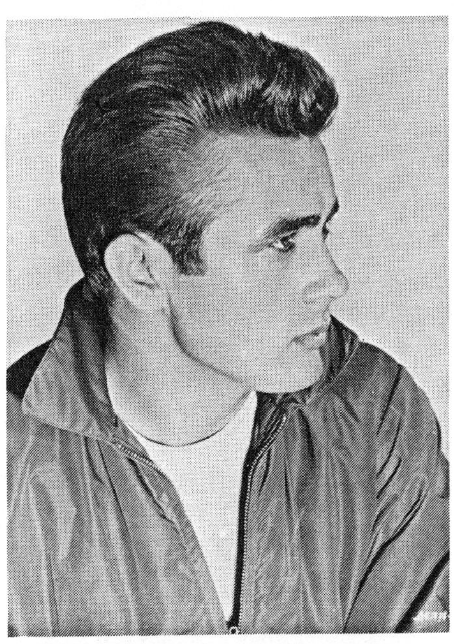

James Dean. He told his friends, "I've had my cock sucked by five of the big names in Hollywood..."

5. WHITTAKER CHAMBERS (1901-1961), U.S. journalist
6. TALLULAH BANKHEAD (1903-1968), U.S. actress
7. HAROLD ROBBINS (b. 1916), U.S. writer
8. ARTHUR C. CLARKE (b. 1917), British writer
9. CARSON McCULLERS (1917-1967), U.S. writer
10. DIRK BOGARDE (b. 1920), British actor
11. MARLON BRANDO (b. 1924), U.S. actor
12. MARCELLO MASTROIANNI (b. 1924), Italian actor
13. RICHARD BURTON (1925-1984), British actor
14. TINY TIM (b. 1925), U.S. performer
15. MICHEL SERRAULT (b. 1928), French actor
16. JAMES DEAN (1931-1955), U.S. actor
17. ANTHONY PERKINS (b. 1932), U.S. actor
18. ROD McKUEN (b. 1933), U.S. poet
19. JOAN BAEZ (b. 1941), U.S. folk singer and political activist
20. GARY GILMORE (1941-1977), U.S. murderer
21. JANIS JOPLIN (1943-1970), U.S. rock singer
22. BILLIE JEAN KING (b. 1943), U.S. tennis pro
23. DAVID BOWIE (b 1947), British rock singer
24. DARYL HALL (b. 1948), U.S. pop singer

15 FAMOUS MEN WHO HAVE PUBLICLY DENIED BEING GAY

1. BOY GEORGE (b. 1961), English pop singer

The androgynous pop star told a London newspaper in 1984, "I'm not gay, and I'm not a transvestite, no matter what anybody thinks. I'm basically very much a man." At other times, Boy George has variously described himself as "bisexual," "very confused," "not confused," and "not really all that keen on sex."

2. ROY COHN (1927-1986), U.S. attorney

The controversial New York attorney, former counsel for Senator Joseph McCarthy and an assistant prosecutor in the case that sent Ethel and Julius Rosenberg to the electric chair in 1953, was asked on *Sixty Minutes* about rumors that he was gay and dying of AIDS. "It's a lie as far as I'm concerned," Cohn replied. Cohn said he was suffering from liver cancer. Later, on the *Larry King Live* show, a phone caller asked Cohn if he was gay. "No," Cohn flatly replied. After Cohn's death in July 1986, it was revealed that Cohn had, in fact, been gay, and had been suffering from "underlying HTLV-III infections." "He denied his homosexuality," wrote one of his friends, conservative columnist William Safire, "because he could never reconcile it with his self-image of political masculinity."

3. TROY DONAHUE (b. 1936), U.S. actor

Donahue told *People* magazine in 1984, "I am not gay. Once in a while people get me confused with another blond, blue-eyed actor who was around at the same time, but it's no big deal. I love women. Sometimes, I guess, too much." Donahue has been married four times, once to actress Suzanne Pleshette.

4. BLAKE EDWARDS (b. 1922), U.S. film director

In a 1983 *Playboy* magazine interview, Edwards was asked if, after writing and directing *Victor/Victoria,* he was worried people would start whispering he was coming out of the closet. Edwards replied that despite having done some typical homosexual experimenting as a child, and despite some fears early in his life that he might be gay, he was nonetheless, in his words, "*very* heterosexual."

5. DARYL HALL (b. 1948), U.S. pop singer

In a 1984 *Rolling Stone* magazine interview, Hall denied persistent rumors that he is gay and that he and singing partner John Oates are lovers. "The idea of sex with a man doesn't turn me off," he said, "but I don't express it. I satisfied my curiosity about that years ago. I had lots of sex between the ages of three or four and the time I was fourteen or fifteen. Strange experiences with older boys. But men don't particularly turn me on. And, no, John and I have never been lovers. He's not my type. Too short and dark."

6. JON-ERIK HEXUM (1959-1984), U.S. actor

Shortly before the gun accident that killed him in 1984, the 25-year-old television star told *People* magazine that while eighty percent of his friends were gay, he was not. He told *Playgirl* magazine: "I would rather people didn't think I was gay, but I don't 'rather' it a whole lot."

7. MICHAEL JACKSON (b. 1958), U.S. pop singer

Jackson held a national press conference in 1984 to refute insinuations that he is a homosexual. Calling the rumors a "terrible slander," he threatened to sue any periodical that printed "new fantasies." Michael's brother Jermaine told one newspaper, "Even to say that he's not gives people the idea that he is. People want to hear ugliness." The Los Angeles *Times* later commented: "There does not appear to be any precedent for a celebrity going to such lengths to proclaim his or her heterosexuality."

8. JACK KEMP (b. 1935), U.S. representative (R.-N.Y.)

As an aide to California Governor Ronald Reagan, Kemp worked for an official who resigned from office in 1967 amid allegations of homosexual conduct. "My name got mixed in tangentially," Kemp told *Newsweek* magazine several years later, "and that little piece of poison just stays there." Kemp has flatly denied rumors that he is gay.

9. PERRY KING (b. 1948), U.S. actor

After playing a gay man in the 1978 movie *A Different Story,* King denied that he was himself gay. "It's funny," he remarked. "Audiences don't think you're a murderer if you play a murderer, but they do think you're gay if you play a gay."

Actor Jon-Erik Hexum. Shortly before his death, he told one magazine that while eighty percent of his friends were gay, he was not.

10. ED KOCH (b. 1924), Mayor of New York City

During the 1977 mayoral primary between Mario Cuomo and Ed Koch, posters appeared throughout New York City with the slogan, "Vote for Cuomo, not the homo." Reacting to long-standing rumors that he is a homosexual, Koch told one magazine in 1982: "No, I am not a homosexual. If I were a homosexual, I would hope I would have the courage to say so. What's cruel is that you are forcing me to say I am not a homosexual. This means you are putting homosexuals down. I don't want to do that." Asked if he had ever had a homosexual experience, Koch replied that he would not discuss his private life in public.

11. CARL LEWIS (b. 1961), U.S. track and field star

Lewis won four gold medals in track-and-field in the 1984 summer Olympics. Responding to post-Olympics rumors about his sexual preference, he told one interviewer, "I could be sleeping with a horse for all they know. I'm not homosexual."

12. LIBERACE (1919-1987), U.S. entertainer

In 1959, Liberace sued the London *Daily Mirror* and one of its journalists for libel, for implying that he was a homosexual. On the witness stand, Liberace flatly denied that he was a homosexual and stated that he had never in his life indulged in homosexual practices. The trial lasted only six days, and Liberace won the suit and a $24,000 settlement. In 1982, Liberace himself became the defendant in a highly publicized lawsuit, which once again called his sexual preference into question. The suit was filed by his former chauffeur and bodyguard, 23-year-old Scott Thorson, who sought $113 million in "palimony" after claiming that he and Liberace had had "an intimate sexual and emotional relationship" for more than six years. Liberace again denied he was gay, and issued a statement asserting that Thorson's suit was "an outrageous, ambitious attempt to assassinate my character." Liberace eventually paid Thorson a $95,000 out-of-court settlement. After Liberace died in 1987, it was revealed that he had AIDS. His homosexuality — an open secret within the entertainment industry — became widely known. Also, shortly after the entertainer's death, the London *Daily Mirror* asked for a refund of the $24,000 libel settlement it had paid him back in 1959.

13. JOE NAMATH (b. 1943), U.S. football star

After he appeared wearing nylons in a series of nationally

televised commercials for women's pantyhose, Namath publicly denied being gay. He told *Esquire* magazine in 1979, "Not only am I not gay, I am not even bisexual . . . I'm sure thirty years from now, if I'm still a bachelor, people will be asking me if I'm gay."

14. RICHARD THOMAS (b. 1951), U.S. actor

In a 1985 interview in *Us* magazine, Thomas denied persistent rumors he is gay. "I think that's been said about everybody," he remarked. "It's just jealousy. People disappointed they couldn't get any, that's all . . . But I have a large gay following and I cherish it."

15. WAYNE WILLIAMS (b. 1958), convicted U.S. murderer

Convicted of killing two of twenty-eight young blacks slain in Atlanta between 1979 and 1981, Williams denied on the witness stand that he was a homosexual, despite testimony that he had once fondled a fifteen-year-old boy through his trousers and had been seen holding hands with another boy on a downtown street. Williams later said he thought homosexuals were "sick."

18 FAMOUS PEOPLE WHO HAD GAY OR BISEXUAL SONS

1. PHILIP II (382-336 B.C.), Macedonian king
2. PTOLEMY III (266-221 B.C.), king of Egypt
3. VESPASIAN (A.D. 9-79), Roman emperor
4. MARCUS AURELIUS (121-180), Roman emperor and philosopher
5. WILLIAM THE CONQUEROR (1027-1087), king of England
6. ELEANOR OF AQUITAINE (1122-1204), queen of England
7. HENRY II (1133-1189), king of England
8. EDWARD I (1239-1307), king of England
9. CATHERINE DE MEDICI (1519-1589), queen of France
10. MARY, QUEEN OF SCOTS (1542-1587)

11. LOUIS XIII (1601-1643), king of France
12. FREDERICK WILHELM I (1688-1740), king of Prussia
13. ALFRED KRUPP (1812-1887), German munitions manufacturer
14. WILFRED BUCKLAND (1866-1946), U.S. film art director
15. EDMOND ROSTAND (1868-1918), French poet and dramatist
16. LADY NANCY ASTOR (1879-1964), British stateswoman
17. LAURA Z. HOBSON (1900-1986), U.S. writer
18. DR. JULES MANFORD (1919-1982), founder Parents and Friends of Gays

7 FAMOUS GAY MEN WHO ALSO HAD A GAY BROTHER

1. SIR FRANCIS BACON (1561-1626), English philosopher and statesman

Both Francis and his older brother, Anthony, were gay. The two were devoted to one another as boys, and remained close throughout their lives. In fact, they lived together for a time, and it was to his "loving and beloved Brother" that Francis dedicated his famous *Essays* in 1597. Their mother — domineering, intelligent, and devoutly religious — was well aware of their sexual inclinations, and sent them both a stream of letters anxiously lecturing them about their health and their souls, as well as their choice of bed partners. Sending an errand boy with strawberries to them one morning, she told them pointedly that the strawberries were theirs to keep, the errand boy was not. On another occasion, she sternly lectured Francis about "that bloody Percy," a man Francis was keeping as "coach companion and bed companion." Anthony's sexual adventures eventually led him to be arrested and charged with sodomy, in France in 1590. Fortunately, his friend, Henry of Navarre — then king — intervened, and the impending sentence of death was suspended. After a long history of physical ailments (neither brother had a strong constitution),

Anthony died in 1601 from gout, at the age of 42. His brother lived on for another quarter of a century.

2. FRANCOIS DUQUESNOY (1597-1643), Flemish sculptor

The Duquesnoy brothers, Francois and Jerome, came from a family of famous artists and were themselves both noted sculptors during the early seventeenth century. They were also both homosexuals. Francois, the older and better known of the two, died in 1643. Eleven years later, Jerome — whose work included commissions for Philip IV of Spain and the empress of Russia — was arrested in Ghent, in northern Belgium, for allegedly sodomizing two of his young male models. Despite his official standing as a court sculptor at Flanders, and despite the pleas of highly placed friends, including the Bishop of Trieste he was condemned to die. On September 28, 1654, by order of the court, he was lashed to a stake, strangled to death, and his body was then burned.

3. FREDERICK THE GREAT (1712-1786), king of Prussia

Frederick had a younger brother, Henry, prince of Prussia, of whom he was enormously fond. Henry, like Frederick, was gay. Henry was fourteen years younger, and Frederick personally supervised his education, making certain he received a broad, liberal background in history and the arts and sciences. Later, as a young general commanding troops in the Seven Years War, Henry performed ably in Frederick's name. In the U.S., during the late 1700s, when consideration was being given to substituting the fledgling democracy with a constitutional monarchy, Alexander Hamilton and James Monroe, among others, suggested Henry as a candidate for the United States' first king.

4. PETER ILYICH TCHAIKOVSKY (1840-1893), Russian composer

The composer's brother Modeste was also gay.

5. A.E. HOUSMAN (1859-1936), English poet

Housman not only had a gay brother — noted playwright Laurence Housman — but a lesbian sister as well.

6. CONSTANTINE CAVAFY (1863-1933), Greek poet

The youngest of eight children, Cavafy had an older brother, Paul, who was also gay. However, because of differences in their characters — Constantine was pampered, introspective, obsessed with ancient history and poetry; Paul was something of an opportunist and social gadfly who spent much of his life in debt – the two were never particularly close.

7. RICHARD LOCKE (b. 1941), U.S. porno star

Locke, star of such popular gay porno films as *Kansas City Trucking Co.* and *El Paso Wrecking Corp.*, has a younger brother, Robert, who is also gay. Once, when Robert was discussing Richard's "performance" in *Kansas City Trucking Co.* with their mother, Mrs. Locke remarked, "Well, I've just come to the conclusion, since Dick's promiscuous anyway, he may as well be getting paid for it." Robert interviewed his older brother in an article, "My Brother, the Porn Star," in *Blueboy* in 1978.

NOTE: According to a 1986 study at Boston University's School of Medicine, gay men are five times more likely than heterosexual men to have a gay brother.

7 SUPPOSED REFERENCES TO HOMOSEXUALITY IN THE BIBLE (KING JAMES VERSION)

1. LEVITICUS 18:22

"Thou shalt not lie with mankind, as with womankind: it is abomination."

2. LEVITICUS 20:13

"If a man also lie with mankind, as he lieth with a woman, both of them have committed an abomination: they shall surely be put to death; their blood shall be upon them."

3. DEUTERONOMY 23:17

"There shall be no whore of the daughters of Israel, nor a sodomite of the sons of Israel."

4. I KINGS 14:24

"And there were also sodomites in the land: and they did according to all the abominations of the nations which the Lord cast out before the children of Israel."

5. ROMANS 1:26-27

"For this cause God gave them up unto vile affections: for even their women did change the natural use into that which is against nature: And likewise also the men, leaving the natural use of the woman, burned in their lust one towards another; men with men working that which is unseemly, and receiving in themselves that recompense of their error which was meet."

6. CORINTHIANS 6:9-10

"Know ye not that the unrighteous shall not inherit the kingdom of God? Be not deceived: neither fornicators, nor idolators, nor adulterers, nor effeminate, nor abusers of themselves with mankind, Nor thieves, nor covetous, nor drunkards, nor revilers, nor extortioners shall inherit the kingdom of God."

7. I TIMOTHY 1:9-10

"Knowing this, that the law is not made for a righteous man, but for the lawless and disobedient, for the ungodly and for sinners, for unholy and profane, for murderers of fathers and murderers of mothers, for manslayers, For whoremongers, for them that defile themselves with mankind, for menstealers, for liars, for perjured persons, and if there be any other thing that is contrary to sound doctrine."

John Boswell's book *Christianity, Social Tolerance, and Homosexuality* (University of Chicago Press, 1980) makes an in-depth study of the likelihood that supposed condemnations of homosexuality in the Bible do not exist in the original texts at all, but are actually the result of later translators imposing the prejudices of their times onto the translations. Boswell has written, "In spite of misleading English translations which may imply the contrary, the word 'homosexual' does not occur in the Bible: no extant text or manuscript, Hebrew, Greek, Syriac, or Aramaic, contains such a word . . . There are of course ways to get around the lack of a specific word in a language, and an action may be condemned without being named, but it is doubtful in this particular case whether a concept of homosexual behavior as a *class* existed at all."

THE 11 U.S. METROPOLITAN AREAS WITH THE MOST GAY BARS, AND THE APPROXIMATE NUMBER IN EACH

	Bars
1. LOS ANGELES/LONG BEACH	105
2. SAN FRANCISCO	95
3. NEW YORK CITY	90
4. CHICAGO	65
5. SAN DIEGO	45
6. NEW ORLEANS	40
7. DALLAS/FT. WORTH	35
8. HOUSTON	35
9. PHILADELPHIA	30
10. WASHINGTON D.C.	30
11 DETROIT	30

21 MAJOR CITIES OR TOWNS THAT DO NOT HAVE A GAY BAR

1. Selma, Alabama
2. Flagstaff, Arizona
3. Anaheim, California
4. Davis, California
5. Santa Ana, California
6. Aspen, Colorado
7. Twin Falls, Idaho
8. Decatur, Illinois
9. Dodge City, Kansas
10. Lawrence, Kansas
11. Rockville, Maryland
12. Duluth, Minnesota
13. Greenville, Mississippi
14. Billings, Montana
15. Helena, Montana
16. Carson City, Nevada
17. Gallup, New Mexico
18. Laredo, Texas
19. Provo, Utah
20. Alexandria, Virginia
21. Laramie, Wyoming

10 MOST COMMON EXPLANATIONS FOR WHY PEOPLE ARE GAY

1. Homosexuality is a genetic trait. It is hereditary and passed on from one generation to the next.

2. Men who become homosexuals were raised in families where the mother was dominant or smothering, and the father was weak or indifferent.

3. Homosexuality is a natural sexual impulse within all of us; because of various complex circumstances, certain individuals simply express it more than other individuals.

4. Experienced adult homosexuals actively recruit young people to become gay, either through seduction or molestation.

5. Homosexuality is caused by hormone imbalances. Male homosexuals have unusually high levels of estrogen — a female sex hormone — in their systems. (Other theories claim that gay men have too much androgen, a male sex hormone, in their systems.)

6. A child raised or treated as a member of the opposite sex will become a homosexual: for example, a little boy dressed up as a girl, or given a doll to play with, is more likely to grow up gay.

7. Social or legal acceptance of homosexuality leads to its spread. For instance, if young people see homosexuality accepted all around them, they'll think it's okay to be gay, and are more likely to become homosexuals themselves.

8. People become homosexuals because they are too unattractive or too shy to make it with the opposite sex. Also, men with small penises become homosexuals because they're afraid to have sex with women.

9. People turn to homosexuality because of a traumatic sexual experience with the opposite sex.

10. Boys grow up to be homosexuals because of guilt feelings or "castration anxiety" associated with having intercourse with women.

8 MEMORABLE SUSPECTED CAUSES OF HOMOSEXUALITY

1. LOUD DISCO MUSIC

A 1979 study at Aegean University in Turkey alleged that male mice continually exposed to loud disco music eventually became exclusively homosexual. The university claimed to have discovered that "high-level noise such as that frequently found in discos, causes homosexuality in mice and deafness among pigs."

2. SMOKING MARIJUANA

In 1986, Reagan-appointed White House drug adviser Carlton Turner announced his belief that smoking marijuana leads to homosexuality. Turner claimed that when he visited treatment centers for drug abusers under eighteen, he found that approximately forty percent of the patients had also engaged in homosexual activity. "It seems to be something that follows along from their marijuana use," he told the press. Similar assertions had been made in 1979 by then-U.S. Senator S.I. Hayakawa (R-Calif.), who claimed that a widespread use of marijuana was responsible for the "huge increase" in homosexuality.

3. ASTROLOGICAL INFLUENCES

The 1933 book *Strange Loves* by Dr. La Forest Potter devoted an entire section to the question, "Are Astrological Factors in Any Way Accountable for Perversion?" "There may be something more than mere coincidence," Dr. Potter concluded, "in the fact that many persons, born under certain aspects, seem to develop sexual abnormalities. In this respect one born under the sign Libra — the balances — seems to be more than usually vulnerable." Some ancient Greeks and Romans also believed that astrology played an important part in determining sexual preference.

4. MASTURBATION

During the Victorian era, masturbation was popularly thought to lead inevitably to homosexual behavior. "Typical" young male masturbators were often portrayed in medical literature as having effeminate mannerisms and developing "morbid attachments" to other boys or young men.

5. VASECTOMY

In 1981, British medical researchers reported the case of a 32-year-old married man who became exclusively homosexual after undergoing a vasectomy. The man claimed to have had no previous homosexual experiences.

6. TOO MANY WOMEN TEACHERS

One early twentieth-century theory suggested that young boys whose grade school teachers were mostly women were more likely to become homosexuals.

7. ATAVISM

Another early theory claimed that homosexuals were genetic throwbacks to man's primitive and amoral ancestors. Some scientists thought they saw this substantiated by the high degree of homosexual behavior among so-called lesser animals, including monkeys.

8. UNCUT MEAT

An aboriginal society in New Guinea believes that men will become homosexuals if they eat the meat of uncircumcised pigs.

11 ALLEGED CURES FOR HOMOSEXUALITY

1. AVERSION THERAPY

The administration of strong drugs or electric shock in order to condition a person to associate homosexuality with fear and pain. While being shown sexually arousing homosexual scenes, the patient is rendered acutely ill by electric shocks, emetics, or drugs that induce a feeling of suffocation or drowning.

2. CASTRATION

Removal of the testicles and/or the penis in order to destroy sexual desire and functioning. Castration was sometimes used in mental hospitals as a treatment for homosexuality and "habitual" masturbation. It was also used as medical treatment or court-ordered punishment for men convicted of so-called homosexual sex crimes. As late as the 1950s, castration was still seen as a legitimate subject for research into curing homosexuality in the U.S.

3. DIET THERAPY

The regulation of diet, nutrition, and bodily metabolism in order to control and eradicate homosexual impulses. For example, one theory held that homosexuality was caused by constipation, flatulence, or other bowel irritations that could be relieved with the proper diet. Another theory proposed that homosexuality was caused by bladder irritations, which could be relieved by eliminating fish and certain other foods from one's meals. Macrobiotics, vegetarianism, megavitamin therapy, vegetotherapy, and other specialized diets have all had their adherents as "cures."

4. DRUG THERAPY

The injection of everything from pulverized lamb embryos to LSD. In the case of English mathematician Alan Turing, convicted of "gross indecencies" with another male in 1952 and ordered to undergo therapy for his homosexuality, the drug was estrogen – female sex hormone – administered to curb his libido. (Among the side effects: Turing suffered impotence, depression, and the growth of feminine breasts. He killed himself shortly after completing the treatment.) Sexual stimulants and depressants, as well as strong general sedatives such as thorazine, have also been used to try to cure homosexuality.

5. "THE LOVE OF A GOOD WOMAN"

Heterosexual marriage, or intercourse with a woman, are still often regarded as cures for homosexuality. In one of the more memorable failures, poet Ernest Dowson took Oscar Wilde to a French brothel to cure Wilde of his homosexuality after he was released from prison. "The first these ten years," Wilde said of his heterosexual experience, "and it will be the last. It was like cold mutton!" In the 1960s, three physicians tried one cure known as the "Masturbation Method:" homosexuals were told to masturbate in an assigned darkened room, and at the moment of orgasm, lights came on illuminating graphic pictures of naked women. It was hoped that the patients would learn to associate orgasmic pleasure with the opposite sex.

6. LOBOTOMY

A form of psychosurgery involving cutting into the brain and severing nerve fibers. Lobotomies were performed as late as the 1950s to "cure" homosexuality. State hospitals routinely performed the operation to control "serious management problems," which often included homosexuals or so-called compulsive masturbators. Between 1940 and 1955, some 50,000 prefrontal lobotomies were performed in the United States. Many of these patients were left in a near-vegetative condition. As late as 1970, a Dr. Fritz Roeder announced that he had "cured" homosexuals, as well as exhibitionists and transvestites, by performing surgery on their brains and destroying part of the hypothalamus gland with electricity. "Young homosexual men," he wrote, "most of them pedophiliacs, are promptly transformed into the straight world."

7. PHYSICAL THERAPY

Rectal and prostate massage. According to some theories, prostate massage kills the "homosexual cells" in the prostate and replaces them with "healthy, heterosexual cells."

8. RADIATION THERAPY

Doses of X-ray radiation administered to various glands in the body in order to alter the functioning of those glands. This was used by doctors who suspected homosexuality of being caused by hormone imbalances or other metabolic dysfunctions.

9. ANAPHRODISIAC THERAPY

The administration of alleged anaphrodisiacs — substances that diminish the sex drive — and the use of various physical devices in order to impair or destroy sexual interest. This has included the use of ice cold baths and penis cages, and the oral administration of saltpeter and cod liver oil.

10. SHOCK TREATMENT

Electrically or chemically induced shock and convulsions. In the 1930s, experiments to find a cure for homosexuality involved pharmacological shock treatment: inducing grand mal seizures in homosexuals by giving them massive overdoses of drugs.

11. TORTURE, EXORCISM, AND DEATH

Torture and exorcism have both been used to "cure" homosexuality. Burning at the stake, hanging, and strangulation were often seen by religious authorities not as punishments for homosexuality, but as cures, since they allegedly released a homosexual from the torments of the flesh and prevented him from committing further sins.

16 UNUSUAL OR ARCHAIC EXPRESSIONS FOR A GAY MAN

1. ANDROGYNE

Used as early as the 1500s to describe a hermaphrodite (a person born with both male and female sex organs), a eunuch, or an effeminate man; later, also a term for homosexuals. From the Greek *androgynos,* meaning literally "male and female in one."

2. BACKGAMMON PLAYER

Eighteenth-century slang in reference to a male homosexual who enjoyed anal intercourse.

3. BIRD

Originally, British slang for a female prostitute, but by the 1920s it also referred to a male homosexual or any person generally regarded as different or outrageous.

4. BUTTERCUP

Early 1930s slang for an effeminate male homosexual.

5. CORNHOLER

Rural American slang for a gay man. From the days when dried corncobs were used for anal hygiene in the outhouse. Chiefly now, when used at all, a term among young adolescents.

6. GANYMEDE

A boy kept for "unnatural" purposes, or a young man beloved by an older man. Also used during the High Middle Ages in reference to any gay male. In Greek mythology, the Trojan boy Ganymede was so beautiful that Zeus, the father of the gods, kidnapped him and made him his cup-bearer and lover. (Later, ancient Roman mythology changed Ganymede to Catamitus, and *catamite* also eventually came to refer to a kept boy.)

7. GENTLEMAN OF THE BACK DOOR

Included in Captain Francis Grose's *Classical Dictionary of the Vulgar Tongue* (1785) as an eighteenth-century British slang term for a male homosexual. A variation was *usher of the back door.*

8. GUNSEL

A young, inexperienced male homosexual; also, the passive partner in anal intercourse. Derived from the German and Yiddish word *gaensel,* which was prison slang for a passive boy kept by another inmate. In the film *The Maltese Falcon,* Humphrey Bogart calls Sydney Greenstreet's trigger-happy young companion, Wilmer, a "gunsel," although by then the expression had also come to mean any petty gangster or hoodlum.

9. INVERT

Popular as a scientific or pseudo-scientific term from the late 1800s up until about the 1940s. Homosexuality was often referred to as "inversion" or "the inverted sexual instinct."

10. LIZZIE

Popular 1920s slang for a male homosexual.

11. MOLLY

In London in the 1700s, there were various raucous men's clubs: The Blasters, The Bold Bucks, The Sweaters, The Mollies, et al. The Mollies, who probably took their name from a common term of the time for female prostitutes, were widely known as homosexuals and were noted for their wild partying in women's clothing. The term "molly" eventually came to refer to any homosexual or to an effeminate man; a "molly house" was a house of prostitution that catered to homosexuals; and a "molly cot" was a prissy or unassertive male. To "molly-coddle" someone still means to pamper them excessively, to the point of emasculation.

12. NANCY

Nancy was English slang for buttocks in the 1800s, but by the turn-of-the-century it meant, on both sides of the Atlantic, a homosexual or an effeminate man. Variations included *nancy-boy* and *nance.*

13. 175-ER

Popular in Germany as a pejorative for gay men during the 1920s and 1930s. Derived from Paragraph 175 of the German Penal Code, which made harsh criminal provisions against homosexual acts.

14. PEDERAST

From the Greek *paed,* meaning boy, and *erastis,* meaning lover; hence, a lover of boys. In 1613, English travel writer Samuel Purchas visited Sicily and wrote in his book *Pilgrimage,* "He telleth of their Paederastie, that they buy Boyes at a hundred or two hundred duckats, and mew them up for their filthie lust."

15. TOMMY DODD

Late Victorian slang for a gay man. Gay men were sometimes referred to as "tommies."

16 URANIAN

Coined in 1862 by German homosexual rights advocate Karl Heinrich Ulrichs, who took the term from Plato's *Symposium,* in which homosexual love was said to exist under the protection of the ninth muse, Urania. In the late 1800s, German homosexuals frequently called themselves "Uranians," and use of the term soon spread to other countries, including the United States. One early homosexual rights group used the slogan, "Uranians of the World, Unite!"

8 ANTIQUE MEDICAL TERMS FOR HOMOSEXUALITY

1. Homophilia
2. Similisexualism
3. Uranianism
4. Mental hermaphroditism
5. Homogenitalism
6. Uranism
7. Intersexualism
8. Androgynism

5 POSSIBLE ORIGINS FOR THE WORD "FAGGOT" AS A PEJORATIVE FOR GAY MEN

1. SCHOOLBOY SEX SLAVES

In nineteenth-century English public schools, "fagging" was the system under which lower classmen were obliged to perform certain duties — such as polishing boots, running errands, or merely obeying whimsical orders — for the upperclassmen. The system was similar to hazing, though often crueler, and it had definite sexual overtones, since it was not uncommon for the younger boys to sexually service the seniors. For example, in his memoirs, English writer John Addington Symonds noted that in his first year at public school, "Every boy of good looks had a female name, and was recognized either as a public prostitute or as some bigger fellow's 'bitch'." To be one of these drudges or sexual lackeys was to be, in the slang of the day, a "fag." The current use of "fag" and "faggot" for gay men may be an extension of this earlier meaning.

2. BURNING FAGGOTS

As far back as the fourteenth century, the word "faggot" referred to the bundle of sticks and twigs used as kindling for burning people — such as "sodomites" and "buggers" — at the stake. Many people now believe that the use of the word "faggot" as a pejorative for gay men originated with this medieval practice of executing homosexuals by burning.

3. SMOKING FAGGOTS

In British slang around the time of World War I, cigarettes were often referred to as "fags." Despite their growing popularity at the time, they were frequently regarded as unmanly, especially compared to a cigar or a pipe, and men who smoked them were sometimes ridiculed as effeminate. As a result, in the popular mind, cigarettes may have come to be identified with effeminacy and homosexuality, and gay men may have come to be called "fags" themselves.

4. GAY SORCERERS

In her book *Another Mother Tongue,* poet and historian Judy

Grahn suggests that gay men came to be called "faggots" because of the word's long mystical association with sacred fire and the sorcerer's wand. She writes: "The faggot as a wand for divination and sacred firemaking has apparently belonged to the province of Gay male wizards, sorcerers, and priests for thousands of years."

5. DISAGREEABLE FAGGOTS

As far back as the 1500s, "faggot" has been a term of abuse or contempt applied to a disagreeable or objectionable woman. The term, in this context, may eventually have been applied to gay men, since homosexuals have often been seen in much the same contemptuous and abusive light as women, and since they have also generally been regarded as disagreeable or objectionable.

6 FAMOUS MEN WHO DISLIKED THE WORD GAY

1. TRUMAN CAPOTE (1924-1984), U.S. writer

Capote complained that the word gay was "inept and inaccurate," and confessed that he hated it. "I do wish they'd come up with something else," he told *Newsday* in 1978. "Even spell it backwards. Even *yags,* I think, would be better."

2. PAUL CADMUS (b. 1914), U.S. painter

In one of his rare interviews, Cadmus told *The Advocate* in 1976, "Maybe I shouldn't say this, it's a word that's used universally now, but the word *gay* doesn't please me. I think it sounds too frivolous. Think of calling Socrates *gay,* or Michelangelo *gay.* Gaiety is a wonderful thing but it does sound as though that were the whole aim in life, as though it were a career in itself. That depresses me a bit."

3. GORE VIDAL (b. 1925), U.S. writer

Vidal told the newspaper *Fag Rag* in 1974 that he had "never allowed, actively, in my life the word 'gay' to pass my lips. . . . It's just a bad word. You see, I don't think you need a word for it. This is what you have to evolve. These words have got to wither away in a true Hegelian cycle."

4. CHRISTOPHER ISHERWOOD (1904-1986), British-U.S. writer

In 1975, Isherwood told *Advocate* interviewer W.I. Scobie that the word gay sounded "coy" to his "old-fashioned ears." "'Gay' is fine as a slogan," he said, "a watchword, a term to describe our philosophy, our attitude toward life. But not, I think, as a title for the movement. I prefer the words used by our enemies. I used to call myself a bugger when I was young. Now I feel at home with 'queer' or 'fag,' when I'm feeling hostile. It makes heterosexuals wince when you refer to yourself by those words if they've been using them behind your back, as they generally have."

5. FRANCO ZEFFIRELLI (b. 1923), Italian film director

Zeffirelli told one interviewer, "I hate to call certain human beings 'gay.' The moment you say 'gay,' I see already a movement or a category or a ghetto. I don't like that at all."

6. JAMES BALDWIN (1924-1987), U.S. writer

In a 1980 interview, Baldwin said, "I spent my season in hell in the gay world, and there's nothing gay about it. I never understood that term. I don't trust any term. I love a few people; some are women and some are men; and it is all much, much more complex than those obscure definitions allow."

19 CLASSIC GAY GRAFFITI

1. Edith Head gives great costume.

2. "My mother made me a homosexual."
   "If I send her some yarn, will she make me one too?"

3. "I am twelve inches long and three inches around."
   "Great, how big is your cock?"

4. If all the gay people in the world got together and planned to go to the grocery store, four of them might show up.

5. Practice makes pervert.

6. Old fairies never die, they just blow away.

7. FCK — The only thing missing is you.

8. Fight heterosexual supremacy — fuck a straight man today!

9. The Pope has decided to exonerate the Jews for the crucifixion; he's going to blame it on the queers instead.

10. Beat me,
Whip me,
Use me,
Fuck me—
But if you mess up my hair, YOU DIE!

11. Young man, well hung, with beautiful body is willing to do anything. P.S. Bill, if you see this don't bother to call, it's only me, Tony.

12. Men that I can't get are men that I ain't met.

13. "Edith Sitwell is a transvestite."
"She's dead, you dope."
"OK, Edith Sitwell is a dead transvestite."

14. I peek while they're pissing
I watch while they shower
Don't want to be missing
A big cock in flower
I'd like to be kissing
One this very hour.

15. There once was a boy named Bill
Who used a dynamite stick for a thrill.
They found his balls
Near Niagara Falls
And his dick and his ass in Brazil.

16. Getting fucked when you have hemorrhoids is like giving birth to a set of broken china.

17. Are you going to come quietly, or do I have to use earplugs?

18. The big difference between my lover and my job is that after five years my job still sucks.

19. Here I sit alone and confused
Tried to hustle but was only cruised.

5 GAY TONGUE-TWISTERS

1. Punk's plump unc drunk punk's spunk.

2. Wong's long dong, long gone, was the wrong long dong all along if the dong you longed fo was longer than Wong's.

3. When the son of Stan comes, the sum of Stan's son's cum comes close to the sum of Stan's cum when Stan comes too.

4. Buddy Butz busts butts buttfucking his buddies' buns, but Buddy's buddies never buttfuck Buddy Butz's butt.

5. Plump Peter Pecker perkily pumped a plumpish pecker, but the plumpish pecker plump Peter Pecker pumped shrunk.

3 MEN THE GAY MOVEMENT DOESN'T WANT TO CLAIM

1. FRANCIS CARDINAL SPELLMAN (1889-1967), Archbishop of New York

Spellman has been posthumously labeled "Superfalwell" by at least one noted political analyst, and a recent biography of him by journalist John Cooney aroused controversy for intimating that Spellman was a practicing homosexual whose sexual conduct embarrassed many of his fellow clergy.

Spellman became a priest in 1916, Archbishop of New York in 1939, and was elevated to Cardinal in 1946. Throughout his career, he exerted an extraordinary influence over American politics, and fancied himself, with good reason, a political "king-maker" in both local and national government; for decades, he wielded power over numerous government political appointments. A close friend and political ally of J. Edgar Hoover, he supported the machinations of McCarthyism during the 1950s, and came to the aid of both Hoover and McCarthy whenever they were under attack. Later, he helped Lyndon Johnson "sell" the Vietnam War to the American people. Spellman called our involvement in Vietnam "Christ's war against . . . the people of North Vietnam," and freely labeled opponents of the war "Reds."

Not all of his political gambits were successful, however. In 1960, he fiercely opposed the election of John F. Kennedy for president. In order to discredit Kennedy with voters, Spellman ruthlessly played on the public's fears and spread bogus stories that Kennedy, a Catholic liberal, was a puppet of the Vatican. Also, when Eleanor Roosevelt publicly opposed taxpayer-financed subsidies for Catholic education (she considered it a breach in the separation of church and state), Spellman publicly denounced her as a "bigot." The Vatican later ordered him to apologize.

Whatever his sexual preference, Spellman toed the official anti-homosexual line of the Catholic Church, and maintained a lifelong conservative stand on all sexual issues. In 1940, he pressured Mayor LaGuardia into dismissing philosopher Bertrand Russell from New York City College, because Russell had criticized Catholic doctrine on sexual morality. Spellman also used his influence to harass Planned Parenthood and other birth control clinics, and exerted political pressure to weaken their funding.

Prepublication galleys of John Cooney's 1985 biography of Spellman (*The American Pope: The Life and Times of Francis Cardinal Spellman*) cited four people who asserted that Spellman was a practicing homosexual whose sex life "was a source of profound embarrassment and shame to many priests." However, the final published biography downplayed these claims, and ultimately hesitated over the subject of whether Spellman was a homosexual or not.

2. J. EDGAR HOOVER (1895-1972), F.B.I. director

Rumors about Hoover's sexual preference have circulated for years, especially since no one has yet unraveled the mystery of his 44-year friendship with constant companion Clyde Tolson, to whom he left the bulk of his $551,500 estate.

Hoover was appointed director of the FBI in 1924, and held on to the post for almost fifty years, largely because of his enormous prestige and political power. "I'd rather have him inside the tent pissing out, than outside pissing in," Lyndon Johnson once remarked after considering replacing him. In 1970, Richard Nixon resolved to get rid of Hoover once and for all, but at the last minute, with the Bureau chief in his office, Nixon got cold feet and instead spent the afternoon listening to Hoover reminisce about John Dillinger, Ma Barker, and the like.

Ardently conservative and morally zealous, Hoover upgraded the Bureau's image and efficiency over the years (it was mired in scandal and ineptitude when he first took over), and along the way he became one of the most feared and powerful figures in Washington. Power went to his head. In later years, he began keeping explicit files on the sex lives of hundreds of private citizens (among them Rock Hudson and other prominent gays), most of whom were not even suspected of any illegal activities. He often used these files to punish people whose politics or lifestyles he personally abhorred.

In the case of actress Jean Seberg, who was involved in various radical political causes in the 1960s, Hoover personally recommended that she be "neutralized." To that end, the FBI leaked false stories to the press that Seberg was pregnant by a member of the Black Panthers. (The child's father was actually novelist Romain Gary, the actress's ex-husband.) Shortly thereafter, the baby was born prematurely and died, and Seberg herself suffered a nervous breakdown. She later committed suicide.

In the case of Martin Luther King Jr., Hoover authorized the illegal wiretapping of King's home, had letters written to King's wife suggesting that her husband was sexually involved with other women, and had a letter written to Dr. King himself pressing the civil rights leader to commit suicide. (Two separate investigations cleared the FBI of any involvement in King's murder. However, it's been alleged that Bureau superiors erased any leads that might have connected them to the assassination.)

From 1950 to 1972, Hoover personally directed FBI surveillance of numerous gay and lesbian activists and organizations, despite persistent Bureau reports that the gay movement represented absolutely no threat to national security. Hoover was particularly upset when one magazine suggested that there were homosexuals working within the FBI, and he directed his agents to harass the writer involved. On other occasions, when Hoover heard rumors that he and Clyde Tolson — the number-two man at the Bureau — were homosexual lovers, he became livid and denounced the perpetrators as "public rats," "guttersnipes," and "degenerate pseudo-intellectuals."

By the time of his death, in 1972, he had become cantankerous, paranoid, and vengeful: a man who almost single-handedly built the Bureau's popular reputation as an efficient bulwark against crime and subversion; and who then, almost just as single-handedly, destroyed much of its credibility in the late 1960s and 70s.

3. JOSEPH R. McCARTHY (1908-1957), U.S. Senator

From 1950 to 1954, in the most militant anti-Communist crusade in U.S. history, Joseph McCarthy and his cohorts belittled and ruined hundreds of innocent people, all of them alleged Communists or homosexuals. His name has since become synonymous with political opportunism and public character assassination.

After failing to ignite the public's imagination with several other lesser political causes in the late 1940s, McCarthy first hit on the idea of an anti-Communist crusade in 1950, and made headlines for himself when he announced, at a meeting of Republican housewives, that he had a list of 205 members of the Communist party working and shaping policy within the U.S. State Department. The announcement was a bluff, but it worked: it catapulted him into headlines across the country.

As chairman of the Senate Government Operations Committee and its permanent subcommittee on investigations, McCarthy (with attorney Roy Cohn at his side) began a four-year anti-Communist witchhunt that employed little more than colorful accusations and clever innuendo. He left behind him a trail of broken lives — innocent government employees were hounded from their jobs, others resigned out of fear — despite the fact that McCarthy was never able to produce the name of a single "card-carrying" Communist in any government department. Various entertainers, writers, and directors were also hounded from their jobs and blacklisted after it was asserted that Hollywood was a hotbed of subversion.

The hunt for Communists was easily extended to include homosexuals. As one Senate crusader, Senator Kenneth Wherry (R-Nebraska), told the New York *Post*: "You can hardly separate homosexuals from subversives ... A man of low morality is a menace in the government..." By the time the witchhunts were over, hundreds of suspected homosexuals had also lost their jobs with the government.

McCarthy, a Republican from Wisconsin, was enthusiastically endorsed for re-election by Dwight Eisenhower in 1952, and he had wide public support for his cause, until his hearings into alleged subversion within the U.S. Army were televised li · ABC for five weeks in 1954. The public, exposed up close to McCarthy's methods, quickly soured on him. Seven months later, his colleagues in the Senate, safely relying on the growing public tide of anti-McCarthyism, finally censured him for conduct unbecoming a U.S. Senator, by a vote of 67-22.

There is now widespread belief that McCarthy was himself homosexual. (It was revealed in 1986 that attorney Roy Cohn was.) Political columnist Drew Pearson discussed the possibility privately as early as 1952. Others have since affirmed that McCarthy was gay. Despite numerous theories suggesting that McCarthy's death was the result of a Communist conspiracy, his death certificate lists the cause of his death as "acute hepatitis, cause unknown."

McCarthy's only legacy to his country was the introduction of a new word into the American language: *McCarthyism,* the making of indiscriminate and irresponsible charges of political disloyalty.

...AND 10 MORE WE'RE NOT EXACTLY THRILLED ABOUT

1. CHRISTOPHER LEWIS

Son of actress Loretta Young. In 1973, he was arrested in California in connection with a child molestation and "kiddie porn" ring involving boys aged five to seventeen. Lewis was charged with "lewd conduct with two thirteen-year-old boys." He pleaded no contest. One detective characterized the defendants in the case as "not homosexuals at all, but sick child molesters who bring discredit to the gay community."

2. VICTOR ARENA

Mafia hitman. In 1985, he turned state's evidence and agreed to testify against reputed mob boss Paul Castellano. In exchange, the government promised leniency for Arena's 23-year-old gay lover, who had been arrested in connection with a series of armed robberies.

3. OTIS TOOLE

U.S. serial killer and arsonist. At the age of six, he torched his first house. At fourteen, he committed his first murder. Between 1975 and 1981, he committed murder and arson with his friend and sometime lover, fellow serial killer Henry Lee Lucas. Police estimate he has killed approximately fifty people. "I think of killing like smoking a cigarette," Toole once said, "like another habit." He killed and beheaded the six-year-old boy whose story was dramatized in the NBC TV movie *Adam.*

4. CARL PANZRAM

Rapist and murderer. He allegedly raped over one thousand young men and boys, killing at least twenty-one of them, before he died on the gallows in 1930. He once said, "I don't believe in man, God nor devil. I hate the whole damned human race including myself." He was thirty-nine when they hanged him.

5-6. NATHAN LEOPOLD JR. and RICHARD LOEB

Thrill murderers, aged nineteen and eighteen. In 1924, in one of the most highly publicized American crime stories of the century, the two boys, both extremely intelligent and from well-to-do Chicago families, plotted to commit the perfect murder. They felt driven by an elitist conviction that their superior intelligence and breeding gave them the right to kill anyone they pleased. Their victim was a fourteen-year-old boy, Bobby Franks, a distant cousin of Loeb. After picking the boy up from school one afternoon, they smashed in his skull with a heavy chisel, poured hydrochloric acid over his face, and then stuffed his body in a drain pipe. Far from being skilled killers, they were remarkably inept; they left telling clues at the sight of the crime, and were soon arrested. They received life sentences for the killing, plus 99 years for kidnapping. In 1936, Loeb was slashed to death in prison in what was later called "a homosexual brawl." Leopold was paroled in 1958, and died in 1971.

7. ERNST ROEHM

One of the founders of the Nazi party, and organizer of Hitler's notorious private army, the "Brownshirts." Roehm's sexual escapades with various young men and boys caused several public embarrassments for the Nazi party. Roehm was once a close friend of Hitler (he was the only man Hitler addressed by the familiar personal pronoun "du"), but Hitler eventually began to fear him as a rival and, during a bloody purge of the "Brownshirts" in 1934, had him arrested and shot through the head.

8. EDMUND HEINES

Convicted killer, who later became leader of the Munich "Brownshirts" under Roehm and Hitler. He was expelled from the Nazi party in 1927 after he called Hitler a "dishrag," but was reinstated in 1931. He enjoyed taking his pick of teenaged sex partners from various Hitler youth groups. He also took delight in killing Nazi opponents by either shooting them in the face or clubbing them to death. During the same bloody purge of the "Brownshirts" that eliminated Roehm, Heines was discovered in bed having sex with his chauffeur; the two were taken outside and shot.

9-10. GUY BURGESS and DONALD MacLEAN

Soviet espionage agents. They handed over British government secrets, from the British Secret Service and the Foreign Office, to the KGB, then escaped prosecution by defecting to the Soviet Union in 1951. After their defection, amid an atmosphere of homophobic hysteria, at least one London newspaper demanded a purge of "both sexual and political perverts" from the government. What followed was one of the worst anti-gay witchhunts in modern British history.

ORDINARY PEOPLE: 7 GAY MEN WHO WERE BRUTALLY MURDERED

1. MARTIN COETZEE

Coetzee was a well-known hairdresser in his hometown of Bloemfontein, South Africa. He was found dead in his apartment on Christmas Eve, 1973; he had been strangled to death with a necktie. Police arrested nineteen-year-old Coenraad Kroukamp, who claimed that Coetzee had plied him with liquor and then made sexual advances towards him. The boy's attorney argued in court, "Although the deceased has been described as a soft-natured person of slight build, he was nevertheless an experienced adult man who had forced himself on a young, healthy man half his age. Who can say what the psychological effect would have been on this young man had the deceased succeeded in his intentions?" Though there were many irregularities in the boy's story — for example, by his own admission he did not at first resist Coetzee's advances — he was acquitted of murder on the grounds that he had acted in self-defense. "It must be accepted," ruled the judge, "that a normal man in his position ... was entitled to defend himself."

2. RICHARD HEAKIN

Heakin, a 21-year-old microfilm technician from Lincoln, Nebraska, was killed by four teenage boys outside a gay bar in Tucson, Arizona, on June 6, 1976. The boys were part of a larger group of teenagers harassing gay men leaving the disco at closing time. Heakin was standing by a car talking to friends when he was attacked and knocked down. Police said his death was caused by a severe blow, perhaps a hard kick, to the back of the head. After the four boys who attacked him were caught and arrested (based on information supplied by witnesses), they confessed to the crime, and admitted they had been out drinking beer and looking "to beat up queers." However, despite their confessions, Superior Court Judge Ben C. Birdsall refused to hand down jail sentences of any kind in the case. Characterizing the youths as "worthwhile members of the community," he stressed that they were all high school athletes and that "none of them use drugs, or even marijuana." He gave them probation, and dismissed suggestions that they at least undergo psychiatric counseling. "The four youths and their parents have been punished enough," he explained.

3. ROBERT HILLSBOROUGH

On the night of June 21, 1977, Hillsborough, a 33-year-old city gardener, was stabbed to death on a San Francisco street by a group of men who screamed "Faggot! Faggot!" as they knocked him down and repeatedly drove a knife into him. His killers had followed him from a nearby hamburger stand, where they spotted him coming home from a date with a boyfriend. Hillsborough was stabbed a total of fifteen times in the chest and face. Of the four men who were eventually arrested in connection with the killing, one was convicted of second-degree murder; another, a juvenile, was convicted of assault; a third received immunity for testifying against the first; and the fourth was convicted of felonious assault. Hillsborough's mother consequently filed a $5 million civil rights lawsuit against the killers. Also named in the lawsuit was Anita Bryant who, Mrs. Hillsborough asserted, had conspired to deprive her son of his civil rights. Mrs. Hillsborough contended that Bryant and other anti-gay zealots, through their inflammatory rhetoric, had created an atmosphere of homophobic hysteria that contributed to her son's murder. (Only weeks before the killing, for example, Bryant had told a large audience of her followers that homosexuals were "human garbage.") Informed of the lawsuit, Bryant commented, "I had nothing to do with any murders. There is a homosexual murder every day in San Francisco . . . my conscience is clear." Mrs. Hillsborough's lawsuit was eventually dismissed by the courts.

4. WAYNE LEE

On the night of March 25, 1979, Wayne Lee, a 33-year-old beauty pageant judge, was savagely beaten in a vacant garage in downtown Savannah, Georgia. The men who attacked him were three U.S. Army Rangers. According to one witness, Lee pleaded for his life and begged the men "Don't hurt me," while they repeatedly kicked, struck, and stomped on him. Lee later died in a hospital without regaining consciousness. The attending physician testified in court, "This was probably the most mutilated person I have ever seen still alive." Lee, he said, was "almost unrecognizable as a human being" when he was brought into the emergency room that night. An attorney for the Army Rangers argued that Lee had provoked the attack by making homosexual advances to the three men at a nearby adult bookstore. He urged the jury to "place the responsibility where it lies," and characterized the defendants as "young, foolish, clean-cut, and honest." Although the defendants could have been convicted of murder or manslaughter, the jury instead convicted them of a misdemeanor offense: simply battery, the least possible charge for which a conviction could have been returned. Superior Court Judge Perry Brannen Jr. sentenced the men to a maximum of twelve months in jail, but left open the possibility that the sentences could be modified to include some kind of community service instead

5. FRED PAEZ

In the early morning hours of June 28, 1980, Paez was shot to death in the back of the head. His killer was an off-duty police officer, Kevin McCoy. At the time, Officer McCoy and a friend were working jobs as security guards in the city's warehouse district; they later admitted that between the two of them they had consumed three six-packs of beer the night of the shooting. McCoy testified that Paez, a 27-year-old Houston gay activist, had made sexual advances to them, including offers of oral sex, and then had tried to fondle him. He claimed that a scuffle ensued and that his .45 automatic pistol went off accidentally, shooting Paez through the back of the skull. Despite McCoy's assertion that the shooting had been accidental, a ballistics expert later testified, "This weapon does not go off automatically." McCoy was indicted by a grand jury on charges of negligent homicide, but was subsequently acquitted. Officially, Paez's killing was ruled an "accidental" death.

6. CHARLES HOWARD

Twenty-three-year-old Charles Howard was known as "Gentle Charlie" to his friends in Bangor, Maine. A slightly built, rather effeminate young man, he was killed on the night of July 7, 1984. He and a friend were walking home from a church meeting that night when they were attacked by three teenage boys, one of whom had suggested to the other two, "Hey, let's kick the shit out of this fag!" Howard tried to run away from them, but tripped over a curb. The three teenagers fell upon him and starting kicking and beating him. Then they picked him up and, despite his terrified pleas of "No, no, I can't swim," they tossed him over a bridge into a stream, where he drowned. The teenaged killers were arrested after they bragged to a friend about what they had done. Originally charged with first-degree murder, they were eventually convicted on charges of manslaughter — a charge of manslaughter legally implied that they did not act out of malice — and were sentenced by the court to incarceration at a youth center in Portland. All three boys were scheduled to be released by their twenty-first birthdays. In 1986, Charles Howard's mother filed a $655,000 civil lawsuit against her son's killers.

7 HARRY WAYNE WATSON

Watson, a 35-year-old Kalamazoo, Michigan man, was sitting by a stream under a train trestle when he was attacked by two drunken teenagers, aged seventeen and nineteen, who kicked and beat him unconscious on the night of May 25, 1985. The boys claimed that Watson had offered them blowjobs and had groped one of tnem. (Watson's friends later said that such behavior would have been "completely out of character" for him.) After the initial attack, the two boys, who were reportedly covered with blood, went off to a party, leaving Watson under the trestle. They returned an hour later with a third boy and a sledgehammer. Their intention was to "finish off" Watson. The gay man was lying senseless where they had left him.

According to testimony, the seventeen-year-old raised the sledgehammer over Watson's head and drove it down as hard as he could three times into Watson's skull. He later bragged to friends that he had killed a "fag," and was consequently arrested. At the trial, an attorney tried to portray Watson as "an aggressive, perverted homosexual who was down there to attack young boys." The jury, which held a prayer meeting before beginning deliberations, took less than two hours to return a verdict exonerating the seventeen-year-old of all charges. In a rare move, the presiding judge publicly disagreed with their verdict. "This is the first time in almost twelve years on the bench," he stated, "that I felt I would strongly have differed with the jury. I would have found first-degree murder." Ironically, the two other boys had already pleaded guilty to charges related to the killing.

4 GAY HOAXES

1. THE UNHAPPY HUSTLER

In 1975, Warner Books published *The Happy Hustler,* the explicit and intimate memoirs of a high-priced call boy. The book featured partially nude cover photos of its alleged author, Grant Tracy Saxon, a good-looking, bisexual "stud-for-hire," who wrote: "The events in this journal all happened, the people are very real. For obvious reasons, the names have been changed. . ." Saxon himself appeared on numerous talk shows, including Donahue. Among other things, he described how he had made a small fortune in the used Jockey shorts business, and bragged that he ran the largest call-boy ring in the country. He also claimed to have had sex with some of the biggest names in Hollywood. His book became a bestseller.

In actuality, however, there was no Happy Hustler, and the book was a hoax. Grant Tracy Saxon was actually a struggling young Hollywood actor, Michael Kearns. The hoax had been dreamt up by Kearns' lover, actor/director Thom Racina, who wrote pornographic novels in his spare time to supplement his income. Racina, who fabricated *The Happy Hustler* from beginning to end, was inspired by the money made by Xaviera Hollander from her bestseller *The Happy Hooker.* When the publisher wanted cover photos for Racina's book, Michael Kearns conveniently became Grant Tracy Saxon. "I submerged myself completely in another identity," Kearns said later, "the identity of Grant Tracy Saxon. I did a Phil Donahue Show. I was flown to Chicago, limousined to the hotel, put up in a lavish room. All my dreams were coming true. And the night before the appearance I was reading the book for the first time!"

Kearns and Racina both made several hundred thousand dollars from the hoax. However, years later — after having actually become a male prostitute, as well as an alcoholic and a drug addict — Kearns said he regretted the whole affair. He compared his bizarre imposture as Grant Tracy Saxon to an episode from the *Twilight Zone.*

2. THE RAPE OF JACK WRANGLER

In a 1976 interview in *Drummer* magazine, porno star Jack Wrangler described how, when he was thirteen, he was gangbanged by the entire swimming team at St. George's Prep School in Rhode Island. He said it was his first experience with sex. He also remarked, "I'm gay and I dig guys. There's very little that is bisexual about me."

The rape story, which became a memorable part of the Jack Wrangler persona, turned out to be a hoax, as did his disclaimers about bisexuality. In his autobiography in 1984, Wrangler admitted that he had been raped, but said it had involved a retired history professor who forced himself on Wrangler during spring break. "I threw the sheets out the window," he said. In the book, he also revealed details of his long-time romantic relationship with singer Margaret Whiting.

3. THE ROCK HUDSON-JIM NABORS WEDDING

In 1971, an anonymous jokester perpetrated a hoax that had cruel and far-reaching implications: engraved invitations to a wedding ceremony between Rock Hudson and actor Jim Nabors (best known as TV's Gomer Pyle) were sent out, mostly to well-known gossip columnists. Copies were soon being circulated throughout the film industry. Hudson and Nabors had been good friends for years (they often appeared together on *The Carol Burnett Show*), and rumors of the "wedding" quickly spread across the country. The invitations were, of course, a hoax, but in terms of bad publicity, it was a grim success. Nabors issued a public denial, but his variety series on CBS was canceled shortly afterward. Actress Dorothy Malone later revealed that Nabors was so hurt and angry that he half-jokingly asked her to marry him to help him get "out of this mess." Hudson's career didn't suffer, but for Nabors it was both a personal and a professional blow.

4. GAYS FOR GLORIA

In 1980, a group calling itself "Gays for Gloria" took out an expensive two-page ad in the *Gay Community News* of Boston. "Gloria" was fashion designer Gloria Vanderbilt, who had recently been barred from acquiring an apartment in New York City's ritzy River House. The ad urged gays to "Support Gloria in her quest for equal housing. Help Gloria get into River House," and gave the New York address of a Jack Campbell for further information.

Not surprisingly, the ad was a hoax. But there was a real Jack Campbell living at the address given. Campbell, who it turned out had nothing to do with the bogus ad or the fictitious organization that placed it, received a deluge of mail from indignant gays. One of them wrote, "How dare you ask working-class gays and lesbians to support this rich, uptight bitch!" Who exactly placed the ad, or why, remains a mystery.

20 FAMOUS GAY OR BISEXUAL MEN WHO SERVED IN THE U.S. ARMED FORCES

1. SAMUEL BARBER (1910-1981), composer: ARMY
2. JOHN HORNE BURNS (1916-1953), novelist: ARMY
3. WILLIAM S. BURROUGHS (b. 1913), writer: ARMY
4. JOHN CHEEVER (1912-1983), writer: ARMY
5. CRAIG CLAIBORNE (b. 1920), author and gourmet: NAVY
6. DAVE CONNORS (1945-1985), porno star: MARINES
7. RICK DONOVAN (b. 1963), porno star: NAVY
8. ANDREW HOLLERAN (b. 1946), writer: ARMY
9. ROCK HUDSON (1925-1985), actor: NAVY
10. RICHARD LOCKE (b. 1941), porno star: ARMY
11. LEONARD MATLOVICH (b. 1942), gay rights activist: AIR FORCE
12. HARVEY MILK (1930-1978), gay rights activist: NAVY
13. MERLE MILLER (1919-1986), writer: ARMY
14. FRANK O'HARA (1926-1966), poet: NAVY
15. PETER ORLOVSKY (b. 1933), poet: ARMY
16. REV. TROY PERRY (b. 1940), founder Metropolitan Community Church: ARMY
17. TYRONE POWER (1913-1958), actor: MARINES
18. JOHN RECHY (b. 1934), writer: ARMY
19. GLENN SWANN (b. 1959), porno star: MARINES
20. TOM WADDELL (b. 1937-1987), decathlon athlete, physician, activist: ARMY

35 MAJOR COMPANIES THAT HAVE ADVERTISED IN GAY PUBLICATIONS

1. Absolut Vodka
2. Amaretto di Saronno
3. Avon Books
4. Beck's Imported Beer
5. Bombay Gin
6. Boodles British Gin
7. Calistoga Water
8. Columbia Pictures
9. Crocker National Bank
10. Dean Witter Reynolds
11. Delacorte Press
12. Dell Books
13. DeWar's Scotch
14. George Dickel Whiskey
15. Doubleday
16. E.P. Dutton
17. Elektra/Asylum Records
18. Embassy Pictures
19. Harper and Row Publishers
20. MCA Records
21. Macmillan Publishing Co.
22. Houghton Mifflin
23. William Morrow and Co.
24. Oppenheimer and Co.
25. Orion Pictures
26. Paramount Studios
27. Perrier
28. Prentice-Hall
29. Remy Martin Cognac
30. Simon and Schuster
31. Stolichnaya Vodka
32. Twentieth Century Fox
33. United Artists
34. Universal Pictures
35. Warner Bros.

DR. LA FOREST POTTER'S 10 CHARACTERISTICS OF THE AVERAGE HOMOSEXUAL

1. Large, easily aroused nipples
2. Mincing walk
3. Sloped and rounded shoulders
4. Thick, "luxuriant" hair
5. Hairless chest
6. Soft, delicate skin ("...acne spots, so frequently present in normal men, are usually absent.")
7. A peculiar swinging motion of the hips (due to anatomical defects in the spine and pelvis)
8. Lack of will-power, perseverance, and "dogmatic energy"
9. A considerable deposit of fat in the region of the hips, breasts, and thighs
10. Abnormally wide hips, "feminine buttocks"

SOURCE: Dr. La Forest Potter, *Strange Loves: A Study in Sexual Abnormalities.* New York: The Robert Dodsley Company, 1933.

DR. LAWRENCE J. HATTERER'S 7 WAYS TO SPOT HOMOSEXUALITY IN BOYS

1. If your young son ... has no really close friends of the same sex;

2. Playing exclusively with dolls;

3. Dressing up like little girls;

4. Exhibiting a reluctance to engage in rough and tumble play;

5. Moving around in a way that we identify as feminine;

6. Showing excessive passivity or submission beyond what would seem appropriate for a young boy;

7. Withdrawal from and fear of expressing assertive or aggressive behavior with their peers.

NOTE: Dr. Hatterer has noted that "no one sign is evidence. You must consider the aggregate of signs, or the cumulative pattern of behavior. And even then, you must not immediately assume that your child will become homosexual." He is the author of *Changing Homosexuality in the Male.*

SOURCE: "How to Spot Homosexuality in Children" by Dr. Lawrence J. Hatterer. *Harper's Bazaar:* July 1975.

FORMER JOBS OF 13 GAY PORNO STARS

1. AL PARKER
Personal aide to Hugh Hefner at *Playboy* magazine; butler; video technician

2. JACK WRANGLER
Child television star with his own NBC series, *Faith of Our Children;* bit parts on *Mod Squad* and *Medical Center*

3. KIP NOLL
Auto mechanic; carpenter

4. RICHARD LOCKE
Tank commander in the army; gas station attendant; insurance claims adjuster

5. ROY GARRETT
   Supervisor in a New Jersey cosmetics factory; bartender

6. KEITH ANTHONI
   Actor in Pepsi commercials; waiter

7. RICK DONOVAN
   Bouncer at a nightclub

8. SCORPIO
   Male stripper; bartender

9. STEVE SCOTT
   Worked in the publicity department at Universal Studios

10. JAMIE WINGO
    Worked in marketing for a gay advertising agency

11. CHRISTOPHER RAGE
    Talent manager for cabaret acts

12. JAYSON MacBRIDE
    Singer and chorus boy

13. MIKE DAVIS
    Theatrical set designer

10 MEN WHO WERE PAID AT LEAST ONCE FOR THEIR SEXUAL SERVICES

1. JEAN GENET (1910-1986), French writer
2. PHAEDO OF ELIS (418 B.C.-?), disciple of Socrates
3. DOMITIAN (51-96), Roman emperor
4. OCTAVIUS (63 B.C.-A.D. 14), Roman emperor
5. ELAGABALUS (205-222), Roman emperor

6. JOHN PAUL HUDSON (b. 1939), U.S. writer and gay activist
7. JOHN RECHY (b. 1934), U.S. writer
8. MICHAEL KEARNS (b. 1951), U.S. actor
9. ALEXANDER MENSHIKOV (1672-1729), Russian general and confidante to Peter the Great
10. AGATHOCLES (361-289 B.C.), tyrant of Syracuse

16 MEN WHO PAID FOR GAY SEX

1. AULUS HIRTIUS (90-43 B.C.), Roman statesman and historian
2. COLE PORTER (1893-1964), U.S. songwriter
3. MONTY WOOLLEY (1888-1963), U.S. actor
4. SOPHOCLES (496-406 B.C.), Greek tragic poet
5. CONSTANTINE CAVAFY (1863-1933), Greek poet
6. MARCUS COCCEIUS NERVA (35-98), Roman emperor
7. CECIL BEATON (1904-1980), English photographer and designer
8. PIER PAOLO PASOLINI (1922-1975), Italian film director
9. A.E. HOUSMAN (1859-1936), English poet
10. GEORGE CUKOR (1899-1983), U.S. film director
11. JOHN ADDINGTON SYMONDS (1840-1893), English essayist and historian
12. WILLIAM S. BURROUGHS (b. 1914), U.S. writer
13. CHARLES LAUGHTON (1899-1962), English actor
14. T.E. LAWRENCE (1888-1935), English adventurer and writer
15. SIR RICHARD BURTON (1821-1890), English explorer and writer
16. SIR ROGER CASEMENT (1864-1916), Irish rebel

13 SEX PRACTICES AND THE PROPER, TECHNICAL TERMS FOR EACH

	Technical term
1. COCKSUCKING	Penilingus, fellatio
2. DIRTY TALK DURING SEX	Coprolalia
3. RIMMING	Analingus
4. GOLDEN SHOWERS, WATER SPORTS	Urolagnia
5. A THREE-WAY	Troilism
6. SCAT	Coprophilia
7. A SEXUAL INTEREST IN CHILDREN	Pedophilia
8. BELLY-FUCKING, THE PRINCETON RUB	Frottage
9. FUCKING SOMEONE'S THIGHS	Intrafemoris
10. SEX WITH THE DEAD	Necrophilia
11. MUD WRESTLING, A SEXUAL INTEREST IN FILTH	Mysophilia
12. A SEXUAL PREFERENCE FOR OLD PEOPLE	Gerontophilia
13. A SEXUAL INTEREST IN ANIMALS	Zoophilia, bestiality

11 SAFE WAYS TO HAVE FUN IN BED

1. MASSAGE

Buy some scented massage oils, light a candle, and give each other a thorough body massage.

2. SHOW OFF

One at a time, watch each other jack off. By doing it separately instead of together, you can focus completely on watching your partner and being turned on by him.

3. SHARE FANTASIES

Have you ever wondered what it would be like to be tied spread-eagled to a bed while a man wearing only a leather jockstrap talks dirty to you and pumps your cock? Or perhaps your fantasy is...

Make a deal with a trusted partner: One evening he'll help you play out any fantasy you want, within the bounds of staying healthy. Another evening, you'll reciprocate.

4. TRY A CONDOM

Maybe you already use them regularly; if you've tried a condom once and didn't like it, don't give up yet. The next list might prove helpful.

5. MIRRORS

Move a large mirror to where you can both see it while you're in bed — or move yourselves over to a large mirror. Whatever you do with your partner will take on a new dimension when you can watch yourselves in the mirror.

6. PHONE SEX

So you can't be with the one you love tonight? Give him a call. Or try any of the many phone-sex services advertising in the gay press.

7. NEW LOCATIONS

Despite the title of this list, sex doesn't have to be confined to the bedroom. What about in the shower ... while taking a bath together ... on the dining room table ... on the stairs?

8. TOYS AND COSTUMES

There's no end to the items that you can incorporate into sex play: jockstraps, blindfolds, cockrings, tit clamps, ropes, leather, vibrators...

9. VIDEO

Do you have access to a video camera? Make your own videos. Helping you with this may be just the excuse you needed to invite a third friend over.

10. FROTTAGE

Try rubbing your cock between your partner's thighs, or in his armpit, or against his chest or stomach.

11. VARIETY

You've heard all (or most) of these ideas before, right? But how many have you ever actually tried? If the answer is less than half – why not use this list as a way to add some variety to your life?

4 THINGS TO KNOW ABOUT CONDOMS

1. Oil-based lubricants will disintegrate the latex of a condom, making it more likely to break or – even if there's no visible break – to allow the AIDS virus to get through. Such lubricants include vaseline, baby oil, cold creams, Lube and Crisco, and should never be used with a rubber.

2. Water-based lubricants are fine. KY jelly, sold in drug stores, is the most popular of these. Others include Probe and Foreplay. These are all sold over the counter, and will be identified on the package as water-soluble.

3. Many men have found that putting some water-based lubricant inside the condom before they put it on greatly increases sensitivity.

4. Different brands of condoms vary considerably. Some men find that natural lambskin types, like Fourex, are best; others prefer latex. An informal survey by *Prevention* magazine found that men rated the Mentor brand number 1. (There is some evidence that lambskin is less effective than latex in AIDS prevention.)

10 SUBSTANCES OFTEN REPUTED TO BE APHRODISIACS

1. STRYCHNINE

Strychnine's rather unlikely reputation as an aphrodisiac is based on its effect on the central nervous system: ingesting a very small amount is said to heighten sensitivity to all stimulation. However, it is an extremely toxic poison. Less than 5 mg. will kill a person, and death is usually the result of physical exhaustion after a series of excruciating convulsions. The line between a stimulating dose and a lethal one is so fine that taking it, even under the pretense of trying to increase one's sexual pleasure, is more a suicidal act than a hedonistic one.

2. CHOCOLATE

Noted sexologist Havelock Ellis believed that chocolate was an aphrodisiac. Unfortunately, there is no evidence to support his belief. Chocolate *is* rich in carbohydrates – as well as protein, phosphorus, and calcium – and is therefore an excellent source of quick energy. It also contains minute amounts of caffeine and theobromine, a diuretic. Its reputation as an aphrodisiac was once so strong that, in the seventeenth century, monks were forbidden to eat it lest their minds become filled with lewd thoughts and fantasies.

3. GINSENG

Ginseng has been used as an aphrodisiac by the Chinese for thousands of years, and has recently gained wide popularity in the U.S. *Panax quinquefolium* is the North American variety, grown mostly in the Appalachian mountain region, but its aphrodisiac effects are said to be considerably less than those of its Oriental cousin, *Panax schinseng.* Most often made as a stimulating tea, ginseng is also said to soothe the nerves, prolong youth, and help the body fight off infection.

4. L-DOPA

The powerful drug L-dopa – levodihydroxyphenylalanine – was first used in the late 1960s to treat people suffering from Parkinson's disease. Today, it is also used, surreptitiously, by some athletes to increase the effectiveness of steroids and pituitary growth hormone. Hypersexuality is a side effect reported in some users. Other side effects, however, include heart disease, skin tumors, and various neurological disorders.

5. SPANISH FLY

Perhaps the most commonly known of all alleged aphrodisiacs, Spanish fly is a delicate powder, the dessicated remains of a southern European beetle, *Catharis vesicatoria.* The Marquis de Sade was infamous for serving guests little chocolate bonbons filled with Spanish fly — a practice that eventually led to his arrest after several prostitutes were poisoned by them. Its alleged aphrodisiac power is an accidental result of its action on the genitourinary tract: it causes acute irritation of the mucous membrane of the urethra and a dilation of associated blood vessels around the genitals. However, it does not, in itself, increase sexual desire. Instead, it usually causes severe inflammation, violent illness, convulsions, or death.

6. HONEY

Honey figures prominently in various Arabic sex manuals, including *The Perfumed Garden* and the *Kama Sutra.* To increase sexual prowess, *The Perfumed Garden* recommended drinking a glassful of honey, and eating twenty almonds, every night, for three nights, before going to bed. To heighten orgasm, it recommended drinking honey spiced with nutmeg. The ancient Greeks also valued honey as an aphrodisiac; honey-sesame cakes baked in the shape of genitals were said to have aphrodisiac powers. Honey is rich in B-vitamins, amino acids, and enzymes. It is also one of the most easily digested foods known.

7. PRAIRIE OYSTERS

Regarded as a delicacy by some (as a gastronomic atrocity by others), prairie oysters are bull testicles, and are a popular item in some restaurants in the Rocky Mountain region, where they are also known as "Rocky Mountain oysters." For the full aphrodisiac effect, they are supposed to be eaten raw and as fresh as possible. Although they contain some male sex hormones, most of these hormones are apparently destroyed in the stomach during digestion. The ancient Chinese and Hindus believed that tiger testicles were also an aphrodisiac. And among some cannibalistic peoples, raw human genitals were ingested for their supposed ability to increase sexual desire and prowess.

8. SARSAPARILLA

In the sixteenth century, sarsaparilla was used, unsuccessfully, in the treatment of syphilis and rheumatism. In the nineteenth century, it was regarded as a blood purifier and as a cure for general lethargy and weakness. Its reputation as an aphrodisiac goes back several centuries to Mexico and Latin and South America, where various parts of the aromatic herb are still used to make invigorating teas and tonics. In the 1940s, a Hungarian scientist living in Mexico, Dr. Emerick Solmo, claimed to discover that the root of the plant contains a chemical similar in structure to testosterone, a primary male sex hormone in humans. His findings were subject to much dispute and derision. Sarsaparilla's primary use in the U.S. has been as a flavoring in soft drinks.

9. VITAMIN E

Vitamin E has been hailed as a cure for everything from varicose veins and senility to cancer and old age. A vitamin E deficiency can apparently cause sterility and impotence in men, but whether or not megadoses of it can improve one's sex life is unknown. Several forms of vitamin E exist in nature, but alpha tocopherol, the most powerful form, is of greatest importance nutritionally. Some of the richest sources of vitamin E are wheat germ, scallops, peanuts, margarine, safflower oil, and raw leeks.

10. YOHIMBINE

A crystalline substance, alkaloid in nature, yohimbine was once one of the most widely prescribed drugs for increasing the sex drive. It is derived from the bark of a tree native to central Africa, where it has long been used by the natives to increase sexual desire and improve sexual performance. Its primary medical use in the U.S. has been in the treatment of neuritis and meningitis. Because it stimulates the lower spinal nerves controlling erection, it has acquired a reputation as an aphrodisiac and has sometimes been used in the treatment of impotence and sexual apathy.

12 SUBSTANCES REPUTED TO DIMINISH SEXUAL DESIRE AND PERFORMANCE

1. Aspirin
2. Cocaine
3. Digitalis
4. Sodium bicarbonate
5. Menthol
6. Potassium nitrate (saltpeter)
7. Hard liquor
8. Tobacco
9. Quinine
10. Lemon juice
11. Lime juice
12. Vinegar

12 FAMOUS PEOPLE WHO BELIEVED IN THE POWER OF APHRODISIACS

1. ARISTOTLE (384-322 B.C.), Greek philosopher

Recommended the use of oil of peppermint to stimulate sexual desire. To reduce the libido, he suggested walking long distances through the hills barefoot.

2. PLINY (A.D. 23-79), Roman naturalist

To fan the flames of lust, he suggested eating a hyena eye with a dash of licorice or dill.

3. NICCOLO MACHIAVELLI (1469-1527), Italian statesman and writer

Often praised the aphrodisiac powers of the mandrake plant and wrote a ribald comedy, *Mandragola,* in its honor.

4. FRANCOIS RABELAIS (1490-1553), French writer
Recommended marzipan, or claret spiced with cinnamon.

5. GIOVANNI GIACOMO CASANOVA (1725-1798), Italian libertine and adventurer
Attributed much of his spectacular sexual energy to the fact that he downed 50 oysters for breakfast every morning.

6. CAPTAIN JAMES COOK (1728-1779), English explorer
The first European ever to set foot on the Hawaiian Islands, Cook feasted every morning on a special, aphrodisiac dish composed of fresh shrimp. He often boasted that he could take on ten native girls a day.

7. MADAME DUBARRY (1743-1793), mistress of Louis XV
She tried to keep Louis XV in her power by feeding him foods that would make him weak with lust: sweetbreads, venison, pheasant cooked in white wine, truffles, capon in sherry broth, to name just a few. "She makes me forget that soon I will be sixty," Louis told a friend.

8. SIR RICHARD BURTON (1821-1890), English explorer and writer
Was especially convinced of the aphrodisiac powers of hashish, and published recipes for making it correctly.

9. HAVELOCK ELLIS (1859-1939), English sexologist
Praised the aphrodisiac powers of alcohol (in small doses), beefsteak, and chocolate. Also believed that perfumes were a powerful aphrodisiac.

10. MAE WEST (1892-1980), U.S. actress
The legendary sex queen recommended eating almonds to increase one's sex drive and improve one's sex life.

11. DUKE ELLINGTON (1899-1974), U.S. jazz musician
Touted both vodka and caviar as aphrodisiacs.

12. TIMOTHY LEARY (b. 1922), U.S. psychologist and LSD advocate
Once claimed that "LSD is the most powerful aphrodisiac ever discovered by man."

7 POPULAR POSITIONS FOR JACKING OFF AND THE ADVANTAGES AND DISADVANTAGES OF EACH

1. LYING ON BACK

Easily the most popular position, illustrated by Tom Cruise in the movie *Risky Business* and Dennis Christopher in *Fade to Black*. Advantages: Good angle for thrusting action with hips; keeps the sheets from getting messy; easy to keep dildo or butt-plug in one's asshole; easy reach for either nipple. Disadvantages: Bad angle to look at pictures; monotonous when used day after day.

2. STANDING UP

Also very popular, especially with narcissists, men who cruise public bathrooms, and guys on the go. Advantages: You can watch yourself in the mirror; easy to do anywhere; convenient to do in the shower where the sound of running water masks the telltale noises you're making. Disadvantages: Knees and legs can get tired and buckle; cum-splotched shoes, carpet, or floor; difficult to keep dildoes in one's ass.

3. LEGS THROWN OVER HEAD

In this position, a guy lies on his back and throws his legs back over his head so that the head of his dick is aimed right at his mouth. Often used in S&M scenes as a way for the master to force his slave to eat his own cum. Advantages: Intense orgasm; great if you're hungry for cum, even your own; sexy position for watching yourself shoot off; leaves ass completely vulnerable. Disadvantages: Sprained neck and back; cum can get in your eyes; difficult position to hold; bad angle for looking at dirty pictures.

4. ON THE BELLY, FUCKING FIST

Advantages: Intense orgasm; most perfectly simulates actual intercourse; good angle for thrusting; good angle for looking at dirty pictures. Disadvantages: Messy sheets; awkward to do while being buttfucked; difficult to reach nipples; parents, roommates, and lovers can sneak up on you without being detected.

5. ON THE BELLY, RUBBING DICK AGAINST SHEETS, PILLOWS, ETC.

Advantages: Good when you're in a lazy mood; good while being fucked up the ass; leaves both hands free to play with nipples or turn pages of magazine. Disadvantages: Messy sheets or wet pillow; cum in pubic hair.

6. ON ONE'S KNEES

Advantages: Most convenient position while sucking cock or eating ass; enhances feelings of being dominated. Disadvantages: "Washer woman knees"; bad angle for thrusting with hips; cum-splotched carpet or floor.

7. SITTING ON TOILET

Portnoy, among others, helped make this position famous, and it was immortalized in the movie *The Right Stuff.* Advantages: Good when you can't find any other way to be alone; towels are right there for clean-up; convenient when you're in a hurry. Disadvantage: Unappetizing location.

9 VICTORIAN "CURES" FOR MASTURBATION

During the Victorian era, masturbation was the focus of extraordinary anxiety among doctors and parents; "curing" it became an obsession. The hysteria surrounding the subject was fueled by righteous moralists who regarded masturbation as a worse sin than adultery, and by quack doctors who claimed that the loss of a single ounce of semen through masturbation was more debilitating to the body than the loss of several ounces of blood. One Victorian-era physician listed no fewer that 47 dire consequences of the act. Masturbation was believed to cause everything from acne and epilepsy to mental retardation and death. Hoping to eradicate this "scourge of young manhood," parents subjected their children to dozens of torturous cures.

1. CASTRATION

Recalcitrant young masturbators were sometimes castrated

to annihilate their sex urge. In some cases, the entire penis was amputated, and voodoo-istic doctors used nightmarish reasoning to console the anguished parents: it was better to cut off a boy's genitals entirely than let him go insane or die from masturbating too much.

2. STRAITJACKET PAJAMAS

Fearing that boys might masturbate in bed after the lights were turned out, some parents turned to pajama tops modeled after straitjackets. A boy's arms were laced into heavy sleeves that were then tied around the back of his body. Other parents gave new meaning to the admonishment "Keep your hands where I can see them," and simply tied their children's wrists to the bedposts every night.

3. ERECTION ALARMS

These were expensive and complicated devices. A flexible metal band was secured around the base of the penis and then attached, with wires, to a small box on the nightstand. When an erection occurred, the penis expanded, and set off a loud electronic alarm. Parents sleeping in another room were notified that their son was on the verge of "abusing" himself — or of having a nocturnal emission, which was considered just as harmful.

4. ENEMAS

Some physicians preached that masturbation was caused by constipation or by a build-up of unhealthy germs in the bowels. They recommended that parents give their children daily morning enemas with ice water.

5. INFIBULATION

Some parents had their sons' foreskins fastened shut with rings, clasps, or staples to prevent erection and masturbation. In extreme cases, the entire foreskin was sewn shut; only a tiny opening was left for urination.

6. BREAKFAST CEREALS

Many Victorian physicians believed that the key to preventing masturbation was good nutrition. With that in mind, they developed a variety of wholesome foods specifically designed to purge a child's body of unhealthy impulses. The American physician and health food pioneer John Harvey Kellogg introduced a

Nutritionist John Harvey Kellogg, inventor of breakfast cereals to help control young men's masturbatory habits.

Courtesy New York Academy of Medicine

new line of such foods at his sanitarium in Battle Creek, Michigan. They were called Kellogg's Breakfast Cereals.

7. DIE ONANIEBANDAGEN

Literally "the masturbation bandage," this was developed in Germany and endorsed by noted sexologist Havelock Ellis. It consisted of a little metal suit of armor that fitted snugly over the penis and testicles and was attached to a lock. The parents of course kept the key.

8. SPIKED COCKRINGS

Cockrings with tiny razors or needle-like spikes on the inside were sometimes fitted around the base of a boy's penis to prevent him from attaining an erection.

9. GOOD CLEAN LIVING

"There is only one way in which a boy can ever break the habit of self-abuse," claimed the nineteenth-century sex guide *Light on Dark Corners*. "He must determine to do it and he must be dead-in-earnest about it. The one supreme factor in the fight is a determined will. A boy can control his morbid curiosity about sex subjects if he will think on other matters. He can drive out the memory of old base pictures and stories and suggestions if he will simply determine to set his mind on the subjects that are fine and clean. And remember, there is no greater single means of help in the fight than to try definitely to help someone else in the same battle. It is wonderful how we get new strength when we try to help a friend break a bad habit that may also be afflicting us. So, pitch in and give a lift to the other fellow, for your own sake as well as for his."

30 PICTURESQUE SLANG EXPRESSIONS FOR MASTURBATION

1. BASHING THE BISHOP
2. CHOKING THE CHIPMUNK
3. COMING ONE'S MUTTON
4. CRACKING NUTS
5. DOLLOPING THE WEENER
6. FISTING OFF
7. FLOGGING THE POODLE
8. HAVING ONE OFF THE WRIST
9. JERKING THE GHERKIN
10. MANUAL LABOR
11. BALLING OFF
12. PADDLING THE PICKLE
13. PLAYING SOLITAIRE
14. POCKET POOL
15. POUNDING THE PUD
16. PUMPING OFF
17. PUNISHING PERCY IN THE PALM
18. SINGING AN ARIA
19. SNAPPING THE TWIG

20. SQUEEZING OFF
21. STROPPING ONE'S BEAK
22. STRUMMING THE BANJO
23. TAKING CARE OF BUSINESS
24. TAPDANCING
25. TOSSING OFF
26. DISHONORABLE DISCHARGE
27. WAVING THE WAND
28. WHACKING OFF
29. WANKING OFF
30. KEEPING A DATE WITH ROSIE PALM AND HER FIVE SISTERS

HUNG LIKE A HORSE: AVERAGE ERECT PENIS LENGTHS FOR 10 SPECIES

	Animal	Average Erect Penis Length
1.	HUMPBACK WHALE	10 ft.
2.	ELEPHANT	5 to 6 ft.
3.	BULL	3 ft.
4.	STALLION	2 ft. 6 in.
5.	RHINOCEROUS	2 ft.
6.	PIG	18 to 20 in.
7.	MAN	6 in.
8.	GORILLA	2 in.
9.	CAT	3/4 in.
10.	MOSQUITO	1/100 in.

16 FAMOUS MEN, ALL REPUTEDLY VERY WELL HUNG

1. LYLE ALZADO (b. 1949), U.S. football player

Alan Thicke told talk show host Johnny Carson on *The Tonight Show* one night, "Whoever said that all men are created equal never saw Lyle Alzado in the shower." "It's an honor," Thicke added, classifying Alzado's endowment as "industrial strength."

2. FATTY ARBUCKLE (1887-1933), U.S. silent screen comedian

In 1921, after a three-day wild party that left the twelfth floor of San Francisco's Hotel St. Francis in shambles, the 300-pound comedian was charged with manslaughter in the death of a young starlet he had allegedly raped. The girl had died of peritonitis and a ruptured bladder, leading to rumors about Arbuckle's supposedly gargantuan endowment. After two mistrials, Arbuckle was finally acquitted of the murder, but by then Paramount had canceled his contract, and his career was finished.

3. MILTON BERLE (b. 1908), U.S. entertainer

Berle's reputation for being well-hung was so well-known that he was challenged to a bet by a stranger who claimed his penis was bigger than Berle's. Berle took the man into a nearby restroom to settle the wager; but despite goading from his friends to show off the *whole* thing, Berle would only pull out enough to win the bet.

4. LORD BYRON (1788-1824), English poet

His reputation as a libertine prevented him from being buried in Poets' Corner at Westminster Abbey, and he was interred instead in a small church near Nottingham, England. In 1938, 114 years after his death, the burial vault was opened, and Byron's body was found to be well-preserved with the features easily recognizable. One observer noted: "His sexual organ shewed quite abnormal development."

5. CHARLIE CHAPLIN (1889-1977), U.S. filmmaker and actor

He cheerfully referred to himself as "the Eighth Wonder of the World."

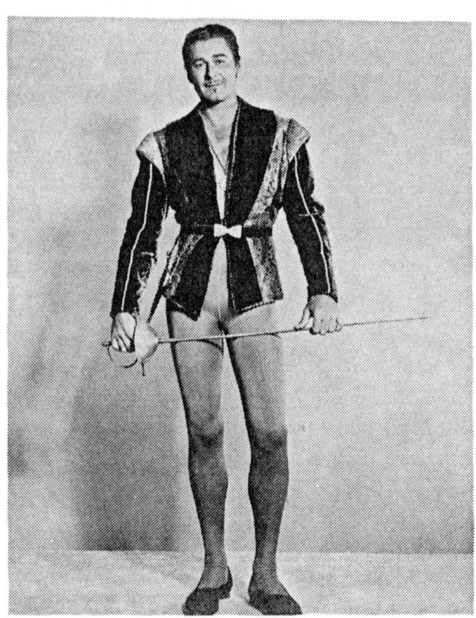

Actor Errol Flynn. If only those tights could talk...

6. CHARLES II (1630-1685), king of England

He was nicknamed "Old Rowley," after a studhorse he owned. It was joked that his sceptre and his penis were of equal length.

7. GARY COOPER (1901-1961), U.S. actor

Cooper's reputation for being exceptionally well hung helped to accelerate his notoriety as one of Hollywood's most prodigious lovers. When Tallulah Bankhead was asked why she was leaving New York for Hollywood in the 1940s, she said it was "to fuck that divine Gary Cooper."

8. JOHN DILLINGER (1902-1934), U.S. bank robber

For years it was rumored that his penis was an incredible 14 inches long when flaccid, 20 to 22 inches long when erect. However, one eyewitness to Dillinger's autopsy later testified that the outlaw had a normal endowment.

9. RICK DONOVAN (b. 1963), U.S. porno star

Nicknamed Rick "Humungous" Donovan, the star of *Giants* and *The Biggest One I Ever Saw* told one gay magazine, "Sure, it does take me ten minutes to get a hard-on, but, Jesus, fellas — give me a break. It takes a half-pint of blood to get this thing up!"

10. ERROL FLYNN (1909-1959), U.S. actor

He was obsessively proud of the size of his penis, and, according to Truman Capote, took it out of his pants at a party one night and tried to play *You Are My Sunshine* on the piano with it.

11. JACK LONDON (1876-1916), U.S. writer

The handsome, muscular writer was often referred to as "the Stallion" by his friends.

12. ARISTOTLE ONASSIS (1906-1975), Greek shipping magnate

He sometimes referred to his huge penis as "the secret of my success," and once dragged an obnoxious reporter into a men's room to prove just how well hung he was. Maria Callas told a friend, "When I met Aristo, so full of life, I became a different woman."

13. GRIGORI RASPUTIN (1872-1916), Siberian peasant and mystic

His penis was said to be thirteen inches long when fully erect. When he was murdered in 1916, at the hands of Russian aristocrats, the oversized organ was supposedly hacked off his body by his killers. According to various sources, the amputated organ was for years faithfully preserved by one of his former servants and lovers, who allegedly kept it in a long wooden box by her bedside.

14. ALDO RAY (b. 1926), U.S. actor

After making a name for himself as a character actor in such films as *Miss Sadie Thompson* and *God's Little Acre,* his Hollywood career started to slide in the early 1960s. He then jumped into the burgeoning porno movie business, where his husky good looks and extra-large endowment helped him find a whole new audience of admirers.

15. FRANK SINATRA (b. 1915), U.S. singer

When his second wife, actress Ava Gardner, was asked what she saw in the "one-hundred-twenty-pound runt," she replied, "Well, there's only ten pounds of Frank but there's one hundred and ten pounds of cock!"

16. HENRI DE TOULOUSE-LAUTREC (1864-1901), French artist

Crippled in adolescence, he never grew taller than 5' 1", but his genitals were unusually large, even for a man of normal size. Referring to his squat body and enormous cock, he described himself as "a coffeepot with a big spout."

6 FAMOUS MALE NUDES

1. PRAXITELES' EROS (4th century B.C.)

Praxiteles' sculpture portrayed Eros, the young god of passion, as a virile and beautiful nude teenage boy. The sculpture — a gift to the ancient Greek town of Thespiae — was so lifelike and seductive that one visitor, Allketas the Rhodian, fell in love with it and masturbated against it frequently, leaving, according to the historian Pliny, the "traces of his lust" all over it. Later, the emperor Nero became so enamored of it that he had it brought back to Rome; it perished there in the great fire of A.D. 64.

2. MICHELANGELO'S DAVID (1504)

Michelangelo was only twenty-nine when he completed his *David*. The eighteen-foot-high sculpture, carved from a damaged slab of Carrara marble, was quickly dubbed *Il gigante,* "The Giant." After the statue was erected on the porch of the Palazzo Vecchio, scandalized Florentines initially stoned it overnight, and in the nearly five centuries since, it has at various times been fitted with a figleaf. In 1975, British novelist Anthony Burgess shuddered at the sculpture's unabashed homoeroticism. "It invokes unpleasing visions of Michelangelo slavering over male beauty," he complained. Michelangelo was paid only about $5000 for the thirty months he labored over the sculpture.

3. CARAVAGGIO'S VICTORIOUS AMOR (1600)

Caravaggio's seventeenth-century paintings have been called "nude pin-ups masquerading as religious works," and during his lifetime Caravaggio was often condemned for the blatantly homoerotic naturalism of his work; some of his contemporaries were outraged at his use of Roman street hustlers and other young gamins as models for revered religious figures in devotional paintings. However, his paintings were otherwise extremely popular, especially with one of his patrons, Cardinal Francesco del Monte, a highly influential papal prelate who was also a renowned pedophiliac. *Victorious Amor* remains the quintessential Caravaggio work, with Cupid erotically portrayed as a naked, seductive, prepubescent boy gleefully trouncing various symbols of human achievement and sophistication. Art critic Michael Jacobs has noted, "The great popularity of a painting like the *Victorious Amor* . . . is proof of how large the market in child pornography was, and how successfully Caravaggio had cornered it."

4. STATUE OF ST. GUIGNOLE (18th century)

In northwest France, a nude marble statue of St. Guignole achieved fame in the 1700s for its alleged powers to cure infertility and frigidity. Desperate women took scrapings from the statue's large penis, mixed the scrapings with water, and then drank the mixture. This created a problem for the shrine's monks who were kept busy constantly repairing or replacing the statue's genitals. Their final solution was ingenious: they drilled a large hole through the statue's groin and inserted a long penis made of wood down through it. As fanatical devotees scraped the penis down in size, a blow with a mallet from the rear would suddenly cause the saint's organ to regain its original length.

5. AUBREY BEARDSLEY'S EXAMINATION OF THE HERALD (1896)

Drawn when Aubrey Beardsley was twenty-three, *The Examination of the Herald* was part of a series of illustrations for an expensive, private edition of Aristophanes' ribald comedy *Lysistrata.* The *Examination* shows a beautiful young messenger boy with a huge erect penis as thick as his thighs and several feet long. The work, along with several of Beardsley's other illustrations for the book, was denounced by many of his contemporaries as shockingly lewd. Oscar Wilde, on the other hand, thought that Beardsley had "brought a strangely new personality to English art . . . Absinthe is to all other drinks what Aubrey's drawings are to other pictures." In the year before his death, Beardsley converted to Roman Catholicism and recanted all of his erotic drawings. "I implore you to destroy all copies of *Lysistrata,*" he wrote his publisher. Happily, his wishes were not obeyed. Beardsley was only twenty-five when he died. In its obituary for him, the *New York*

The Examination of the Herald. Aubrey Beardsley, 1896. It shows what one critic has called "Beardsley's open and provocative obsession with the penis."

Times dismissed his work as "a passing fad," and confidently predicted: "A coming age will wonder why there was any brief interest taken in Beardsley's work."

6. CENTERFOLD OF BURT REYNOLDS (1972)

Riding high on a growing wave of sexual liberation for women, *Cosmopolitan* published the first mainstream nude centerfold of a man, in April 1972: a photograph of "macho" movie star Burt Reynolds, then thirty-six, naked (except for his genitals coyly-covered) on a tiger-skin rug. Reynolds' picture cleared the way for "beefcake" magazines for women, notably *Playgirl* and *Viva.* The issue with Reynolds's centerfold was touted as the largest-selling issue of any magazine in publishing history. Across the ocean, the English edition of *Cosmopolitan* also featured a nude centerfold that month: not of Burt Reynolds, but of feminist Germaine Greer's husband, construction worker Paul de Feu. De Feu described his posing as "striking a blow for male servitude."

15 EIGHTEENTH-CENTURY SLANG EXPRESSIONS FOR COCK

1. CREAMSTICK
2. DIRK
3. FLUTE
4. JOCK
5. LEATHER STRETCHER
6. LOBCOCK
7. PEACEMAKER
8. PIKESTAFF
9. PILGRIM'S STAFF
10. PLUG-TAIL
11. PLUM-TREE SHAKER
12. PUMP HANDLE
13. RUMP-SPLITTER
14. STAR-GAZER
15. SUGARSTICK

20 NINETEENTH-CENTURY SLANG EXPRESSIONS FOR COCK

1. BABY-MAKER
2. BUSHWHACKER
3. CRANNY HUNTER
4. DINGLE-DANGLE
5. GRAVY GIVER
6. HIS MAJESTY IN PURPLE CAP
7. JIGGLING BONE
8. JOHN THOMAS
9. LITTLE BROTHER
10. LOLLIPOP
11. MAN-ROOT
12. NATURE'S SCYTHE
13. OLD SLIMY
14. PILE-DRIVER
15. PISTOL
16. RAMMER
17. TROUSER SNAKE
18. WATERWORKS
19. WINKLE
20. YUM-YUM

THE ORIGINS OF 7 COMMON SEX-RELATED WORDS

1. TESTICLES

In ancient Rome, the word "testari" meant to be a witness. A derivative of the word — "testes" — came to refer to a man's testicles, since these were a witness to his manhood. Testimony, testament, and testify were all derived from the same root as *testicles.*

2. PENIS

Penis shares the same origin as the words pencil and penicillin. All are derived from the Latin "penis," which meant a tail.

3. COCK

As a synonym for "penis," the word *cock* dates back at least to the sixteenth century. It was likely derived from an earlier and still current use of the word to mean a spout or short pipe through which liquid passes. In a sexual context, it was not really considered lewd or impolite until the early 1800s. It can be found in Shakespeare's *Henry V* (1599): "Pistol's cock is up, and flashing fire will follow." Laurence Olivier's 1945 film version of the play retained the line, but the censors of the day were either too ignorant or, less probably, too enlightened to object to it.

4. SEMEN

Semen is derived from the Latin "semen," meaning seed. The word "seminary" – a place where intellectual seeds are sown – also came from "semen."

5. DICK

Dick probably came from the older English word "dirk," meaning a small sword. "Dirk," in turn, was derived from "dorke," meaning the horns of an animal. "Dirk" and "dork" were also once slang expressions for the penis.

6. COME, CUM

The origin of *come* for semen is not exactly known. As a verb, *come* has had a sexual sense at least since the sixteenth century, when the phrases "come at" and "come in unto" referred to sexual intercourse. In the nineteenth century, *come,* again as a verb, referred to the highly suggestive context of butter forming in a churn: the butter had *come;* that is, it had formed. Another possible connection is the seventeenth-century English word "coome," which referred to a kind of very sweet honey. The alternate spelling *cum* probably originated with writers and editors who wanted an easy way for the eye to distinguish it from the more common verb "to come."

7. MASTURBATE

There are two theories of where the word *masturbate* comes from. One holds that it is derived from the Latin words "mazdo," meaning penis, and "turba," meaning agitation: agitation of the penis. Another claims that it is from the Latin words "manus," meaning hand, and "stuprare," meaning defilement: to defile oneself with one's hand.

10 WORDS OR PHRASES THAT SOUND OBSCENE, BUT AREN'T

1. TONGUER
   One who makes or inserts the tongues of shoes.

2. CUNTLINES
   The indented spiral intervals formed between the strands of a rope.

3. BUNGHOLE
   The hole in a cask, through which it is emptied or filled.

4. COCKHEAD
   The top of a grinding-mill spindle.

5. TITMAN
   The runt in a litter of pigs.

6. PRICK SHOOTING
   Shooting with bow and arrow at a fixed mark.

7. BUTTSTRAP
   In carpentry, a strap or plate covering a butt joint.

8. DICK-ASS
   A donkey.

9. COCKMASTER
   A trainer or breeder of game cocks.

10. ARMPIT SNIFFER
    A person employed to test the effectiveness of deodorants by sniffing the armpits of test subjects.

12 PROVOCATIVELY NAMED BUSINESSES

1. B&D SUPERMARKET (South Carolina)
2. GAY DRUGS (Redford, Michigan)
3. YOUNGER COCK TAVERN (London, England)
4. DICK'S DRILLING (Amarillo, Texas)
5. SALTY SEAMAN TAVERN (Columbus, Ohio)
6. QUEEN CITY TIRE (Allentown, Penn.)
7. S&M FIXTURES AND CABINETS (Minneapolis)
8. BUN BOY MOTEL (Southern California)
9. RIM CAFE (Heber, Arizona)
10. KUM-N-GO MARKET (Glendale, Arizona)
11. DYKELAND CENTER (Sterling Heights, Michigan)
12. GOLDEN SPREAD PUMPING SERVICE (Amarillo, Texas)

17 FAMOUS PEOPLE WHO HAD SYPHILIS

1. CHARLES BAUDELAIRE (1821-1867), French poet
2. AL CAPONE (1899-1947), U.S. gangster
3. CHRISTOPHER COLUMBUS (1451-1506), Italian explorer
4. ISAK DINESEN (1885-1962), Danish writer
5. ALEXANDER DUMAS père (1802-1870), French writer
6. PAUL GAUGUIN (1848-1903), French painter
7. FRANCISCO DE GOYA (1746-1828), Spanish painter
8. HENRY VIII (1491-1547), king of England
9. JAMES JOYCE (1882-1941), Irish writer
10. GUY DE MAUPASSANT (1850-1893), French writer
11. BENITO MUSSOLINI (1883-1945), Italian dictator

12. FRIEDRICH NIETZSCHE (1844-1900), German philosopher
13. PETER THE GREAT (1672-1725), tsar of Russia
14. ARTHUR SCHOPENHAUER (1788-1860), German philosopher
15. HENRI DE TOULOUSE-LAUTREC (1864-1901), French artist
16. PAUL VERLAINE (1844-1896), French poet
17. OSCAR WILDE (1854-1900), Irish dramatist and wit

4 MEN IT WOULD HAVE BEEN BETTER NOT TO GO HOME WITH

1. FRITZ HAARMANN (1876-1924)

Otherwise known as the "Hanover Vampire," Haarmann spent much of his life in and out of trouble, for child-molesting, public indecency, and lewd conduct. Then he met and fell under the spell of a young down-and-out male prostitute, Hans Grans. Grans had a violent temper and a passion for the macabre, and Haarmann was so in love with the boy that he could refuse him nothing. Working together between 1918 and 1924, the two of them murdered upwards of fifty young men and boys in the city of Hanover, Germany. Grans chose the victims (in one case, he coveted a pair of pants a boy was wearing), and, as one newspaper later put it, all of the victims were literally "bitten to death." In most cases, the boys were lured to Haarmann's cookshop, where they were quickly overpowered and knocked to the floor. Haarmann and Grans then fell upon the victim's throat, eating the neck and part of the head while frantically stimulating each other to orgasm. The victim was usually still alive during much of the ordeal.

Because of his vocation as a butcher, Haarmann made hundreds of people in the city unwitting accessories to his cannibalism: after killing his victims, he butchered their bodies and sold the remains as meat pies, soup bones, steaks, sausages, and other cuts of meat. After World War I, the city was suffering from famine, and it was often noted with puzzlement that Haarmann's shop had a steady supply of fresh meat when other shops in the area had none. Haarmann and Grans were eventually apprehended and brought to trial. (A third sometime-accomplice was never caught.) Grans received a sentence of life imprisonment, later commuted to twelve years. Haarmann was condemned to death by decapitation. After his execution, his brain was removed and sent to a university for a study into the criminally insane. Ulli Lommel's 1973 film *Tenderness of the Wolves,* produced by Rainer Werner Fassbinder, was inspired by Haarmann's case.

2. DEAN ALLEN CORLL (1940-1973)

To one of the people who knew him in Houston, Texas, Dean Allen Corll was "the nicest person you'll ever meet with the most infectious smile you'll ever see." To another, he was a "nice, polite man who loved to be around kids." The 33-year-old Corll had served in the Army, had once run a local candy store, and worked as an electrician for the Houston Lighting and Power Co. He was also the key figure behind one of the worst killing sprees, lasting from 1970 to 1973, in U.S. history. With the help of two teenage accomplices (who were paid from $5 to $10 for each victim they helped round up), Corll lured adolescent boys, most of them runaways, to glue- and paint-sniffing parties at his suburban home. Once there, the victims were drugged, gagged, stripped naked, and tied down to a specially constructed plywood "torture" plank. A plastic sheet was spread beneath the victims to catch their blood. Corll then raped and mutilated them. Some were tortured for days before Corll finally strangled them or shot them through the head with his .22 pistol, or before they died of shock. Others were dispatched in as little as ten minutes. "It's probably safe to say," said one psychiatrist, "that after the first murder Corll saw it was easy to kill, and the rest of his victims were not people to him, they were like dolls." In all, police eventually uncovered the bodies of twenty-seven victims, though suspicions remain that there were more. (Corll once bragged that he had also done a fair amount of killing in California.) Corll's killing spree ended when one of his accomplices, a seventeen-year-old high school dropout, shot him to death in self-defense; Corll was apparently incensed when the boy brought home a fifteen-year-old female victim for a change.

3. JOHN WAYNE GACY JR. (b. 1942)

In 1968, Gacy was convicted of a sodomy charge involving a teenage boy; he was sentenced to ten years in prison, but was paroled after eighteen months. In 1971, he was accused of raping a 27-year-old man, but charges were dropped when the victim failed to show up in court. Then, in 1978, police traced a missing fifteen-year-old boy to Gacy's home in suburban Chicago. Shortly thereafter, the digging began. "The only thing they can get me for is running a funeral parlor without a license," Gacy quipped as police unearthed body after body from beneath his home.

Outwardly, in some ways, Gacy seemed an unlikely candidate for mass murderer. The owner of a small construction company, he earned over $200,000 a year and was a member of the Jaycees. In 1970, he became a Democratic precinct captain. He enjoyed dressing up as Pogo the Clown and entertaining children in charity shows at local hospitals, and he had received awards for his many civic contributions. But slightly more than a year after the digging under his house began, Gacy was convicted of murdering more people than anyone else in U.S. history: thirty-three young men and boys, whom he had raped, tortured, and killed between January 1972 and December 1978. Police found most of the bodies, nine of them still unidentified, buried in a forty-foot crawlspace beneath the house. (Gacy's second wife, who divorced him in 1976, once complained about an unpleasant odor coming from underneath the house; he told her it was the smell of dead rats.) Some of the victims were slowly strangled with a tourniquet around their necks; Gacy liked to prolong his victim's agony. Others were savagely tortured, and Gacy leaned over them reading loudly from the Bible while they convulsed.

Gacy eventually confessed to the murders. But then, in 1982, while he was awaiting execution on Menard Prison's death row, he did a macabre about-face and told a newspaper interviewer that someone else must have put all of those bodies under his house. In the same interview, Gacy desperately tried to portray himself as a gentle, kind, religious man. "I have never been a homosexual," he added. "My own doctors say just the opposite. They say I have a strong hatred toward them." About his victims, he remarked: "When I read that nineteen of them were prostitutes, I ask: What happened to the family unit?" Gacy's death sentence is still under appeal. Said the father of the fifteen-year-old boy whose disappearance led police to Gacy's home to begin with, "I'll go down and pull the switch myself if they want me to."

4. WILLIAM G. BONIN (b. 1947)

Bonin, a husky, good-looking 34-year-old truck driver, was described by friends as having a hypnotic, dominating personality. He lived with his parents in a suburb of Los Angeles, was frequently unemployed, and attracted little attention to himself – until, in July 1980, he was arrested as the ringleader behind the so-called "Freeway Killings" in Los Angeles. Beginning in the mid-1970s, the bodies of numerous young men and boys, forty-four in all, were found beside freeways in parts of Los Angeles County and neighboring Orange County. Bonin, a muscular drifter with a previous conviction for child molestation, was subsequently charged with twelve of the killings, though police clearly suspected his involvement in many more. (Bonin himself told a television newsman that he had killed at least twenty-one youths.) Three young accomplices, two of them teenagers, were charged with complicity in the murders. One later hanged himself in jail before the case went to trial.

According to testimony, Bonin, sometimes with friends, cruised the streets in his "death van," and picked up hitchhikers, hustlers, and other young men. Once inside the van, the victims were robbed, raped, brutally tortured, and, finally, put to death. Bonin then dumped their bodies beside various freeways in the Los Angeles area. His youngest victim was twelve. One thirteen-year-old boy was castrated before he died. Another victim was killed with an icepick driven into his skull. Others were strangled with their t-shirts. And still another, a seventeen-year-old German tourist named Marcus Grabs, was stabbed seventy times. "I can only liken it to a rabid dog that has gone mad and does not know when to stop biting," one homicide investigator said of the Grabs killing. Bonin was convicted in ten of the murders; he later stood trial for four more. With mothers and other relatives of some of the victims sitting in the front row of the court, Judge William Keene sentenced him to death. Bonin is still awaiting execution.

19 MALE SEX SYMBOLS AND HOW OLD EACH WILL BE IN 1988

	Age
1. MARLON BRANDO	64
2. PAUL NEWMAN	63
3. STEVE REEVES	62
4. CLINT EASTWOOD	58
5. ROD TAYLOR	58
6. TAB HUNTER	57
7. WILLIAM SHATNER	57
8. GEORGE MAHARIS	55
9. ED BYRNES	55
10. RICHARD CHAMBERLAIN	53
11. ROBERT CONRAD	53
12. TROY DONAHUE	52
13. DAVID NELSON	52
14. BURT REYNOLDS	52
15. WARREN BEATTY	50
16. HARRISON FORD	46
17. MICK JAGGER	45
18. JAN-MICHAEL VINCENT	44
19. TOM SELLECK	43

Marlon Brando (right) in *The Wild One* (1954). Brando was born April 3, 1924, in Omaha, Nebraska. Actor Brandon De Wilde (left). Julie Harris, who co-starred with him in *A Member of the Wedding*, called him "the most beautiful, loving, golden child . . . a real artist." De Wilde died in a car accident during a thunderstorm outside Denver when he was thirty.

8 HEARTTHROBS FROM THE PAST AND HOW OLD EACH WOULD BE IF HE WERE ALIVE IN 1988

	Age
1. ERROL FLYNN	79
2. MONTGOMERY CLIFT	68
3. STEVE McQUEEN	58
4. JAMES DEAN	57
5. NICK ADAMS	57
6. SAL MINEO	49
7. RICKY NELSON	48
8. BRANDON DE WILDE	46

12 EXAMPLES OF GAYS ON NETWORK TELEVISION

1. CBS REPORTS: THE HOMOSEXUALS (CBS), 1967

Host Mike Wallace interviewed five homosexuals. The show was originally proposed in 1965, but didn't get on the air until two years later. The producers attempted to give a candid and, in their minds, balanced view of homosexuality by interviewing two men who were happy with their lifestyle, another who was ambivalent and confused, and two others who were deeply troubled. All five men were interviewed behind potted palm trees so that their faces were obscured. Also included were interviews with two psychiatrists, both of whom presented a grim view of homosexual life. "The average homosexual," Wallace reported, "if there be such, is promiscuous. He's not interested in, nor capable of, a lasting relationship like that of a heterosexual marriage."

Despite the inclusion of these unfavorable viewpoints, network executives still found the completed documentary too positive in its approach. Strategic cuts, which rearranged and distorted the remarks of one of the "healthy" interviewees, were made in an effort to give the program a more disparaging tone. The resulting program was heavily biased and strongly disapproving, but it aired only once: the man whose remarks had been tampered with filed a formal complaint against CBS, citing fraud, and withdrew his release, effectively freezing all reruns of the show.

2. N.Y.P.D. (ABC), 1967

N.Y.P.D. prided itself on being a gritty, realistic police action series. The scripts were supposedly based on actual cases from the New York Police Department. In 1967, in what was television's first dramatic treatment of homosexuality, detectives Haines, Ward, and Corso (played by series regulars Jack Warden, Robert Hooks, and Frank Converse) tracked down and broke up a hotel extortion ring that preyed on homosexuals. It was the first time the word "homosexual" was used on television in a dramatic context.

3. THAT CERTAIN SUMMER (ABC), 1972

In an ABC made-for-TV movie, Hal Holbrook and Martin

Sheen played gay lovers dealing with a visit from Holbrook's fourteen-year-old son. During the visit, the boy learns the truth about his father's sexuality. Regarded by most critics at the time as an honest treatment of a complex and sensitive subject, it was criticized by many gay activists. Author John Rechy complained, "It was crumbs. It was safe. They chose the safest types; they didn't take a marvelous queen, a radical queen, a promiscuous homosexual. They chose the closest they could come to middle-class America."

The lovers in the show never touched, except once when Sheen gave Holbrook a reassuring pat on the shoulder, and ABC caved in to pressure to have Holbrook's character remark to his son, "A lot of people — most people, I guess — think it's wrong. They say it's a sickness, that it's something that has to be cured. I don't know. I do know that it isn't easy. If I had a choice, it's not something I'd pick for myself." Gay media activist Ronald Gold told the network, "You're violating your own tradition by compromising with bigotry. You wouldn't have a black character saying, 'I don't know if I'm lazy and shiftless,' or give the Ku Klux Klan equal time to represent its point of view. But you have gays saying, 'I don't know if I'm sick,' and you pay careful attention to the Anita Bryants."

4. MARCUS WELBY, M.D. (ABC), 1973

In an episode entitled "The Other Martin Loring," a young husband confessed to Dr. Welby that he was gay. Welby assured him that with proper psychiatric care, he could be cured.

5. MARCUS WELBY, M.D. (ABC), 1974

Another Welby episode, "The Outrage," provoked a nationwide protest. The show was about a male science teacher who rapes a fourteen-year-old boy. The show was condemned for singling out homosexuals as child molesters when, as critics pointed out, over ninety percent of the child sexual abuse in the country is heterosexual. In response to a campaign spearheaded by gay activists, who acquired a copy of the script before the show was aired, five stations, led by ABC's Boston affiliate, agreed not to broadcast the program because it fostered "a false and negative stereotype of homosexuals"; eight more affiliates broadcast disclaimers or made time available for gay rebuttals; and seven major sponsors pulled their advertising from the show. After receiving a letter of complaint from the National Gay Task Force, an executive at Universal Studios (which had produced the program) angrily, and erroneously, asserted, "If as you indicate, there are 20 million homosexuals in America, then there must be at least 180 million heterosexuals. To our knowledge not one heterosexual has ever pressured us or attempted to dictate program content." However, ABC eventually agreed not to rerun the episode.

6. POLICE WOMAN (NBC), 1974

An episode called "Flowers of Evil" featured three murderous lesbians who kill residents of the Golden Years Retirement Home for their money. Fearing the kind of offensive launched in response to Marcus Welby's "The Outrage," NBC decided to shelve the episode without airing it, then said it would air the program with all references to lesbianism deleted. However, when the show finally appeared, no deletions were apparent: the killers' lesbianism was intact. NBC used various pressure tactics to make certain no affiliates pre-empted the show, as some of ABC's affiliates had done with "The Outrage."

The program's producer, David Gerber, later commented, "That was a tough-minded show about homicidal maniacs who happened to be homosexual. That's honest. That's realistic." The show touched off protest demonstrations in several cities and a sit-in at NBC's headquarters in Burbank. In 1975, NBC announced that the episode would not be rerun, and agreed to work more closely with gay media consultants in the future.

7. SOAP (ABC), 1977

ABC received 32,000 letters of protest about *Soap* – *before* it went on the air. Billed as a satire of soap operas and as a comedy of contemporary sexual mores, the series was condemned by conservative and religious groups, including the National Council of Churches, as "a deliberate effort . . . to tear down our moral values." They urged sponsors to boycott the show. One of the main objections was to the inclusion in the series of an on-going gay character, Jodie, played by comedian Billy Crystal.

Some gay activists, it turned out, were also upset about the character, but for entirely different reasons. When word got out that Jodie was to be an effeminate gay man who dresses in his mother's clothes and desires a sex change operation, a group calling itself the International Union of Gay Athletes threatened to stage nationwide protests. Claiming a membership of over 450 gay and bisexual collegiate athletes, the IUGA successfully negotiated with ABC to have Jodie developed into a more masculine character and to provide him with an all-American football player lover. The IUGA gambit was something of an inspired bluff: far from having a membership of 450 athletes, the group consisted of only four members and a fictitious leader. *Soap* was phenomenally successful in its first two seasons, despite the calls to boycott it, but by the second season Jodie had become bisexual and had fathered a son.

8. A QUESTION OF LOVE (ABC), 1978

Gena Rowlands portrayed a lesbian mother involved in an ugly custody battle for her young son. The made-for-TV movie was based on an actual court case of a mother who lost custody of her children because she was living with another woman. Believing that the general public had a more tolerant view of lesbianism than of male homosexuality, the program's producers wanted to highlight the physical relationship between Rowlands' character and her live-in lover (Jane Alexander), but were finally allowed only to show such intimacies as one of the women drying the other's hair.

9. GAY POWER, GAY POLITICS (CBS), 1980

Thirteen years after its first documentary on homosexuality, CBS approached the subject again, this time with *Gay Power, Gay Politics,* an hour-long special on the growing political power of gays in San Francisco. Despite its title, the documentary did not mention gay civil rights legislation, job or housing discrimination, or any of the other major political concerns of gays in San Francisco, and neither Mayor Diane Feinstein nor the city's only openly gay, elected supervisor, Harry Britt, were interviewed. (According to reports, the show's producer was kicked out of Feinstein's office after he tried to initiate an "outrageous and unprofessional" interview with her.)

Instead, CBS chose to focus on gay public sex acts, transvestism, and the gay S&M scene. Producer/reporter George Crile compared life in San Francisco to decadent, pre-Nazi Berlin. "The camera never got above the crotch level," complained one gay activist who had been interviewed for the program. After the show was aired, the National Gay Task Force filed a complaint against CBS with the National News Council, an impartial news monitoring agency. The NNC later strongly criticized CBS for the program and concluded that "by concentrating on certain flamboyant examples of homosexual behavior, the program tended to reinforce stereotypes." CBS made an apology about only one specific misrepresentation: they admitted they had doctored the soundtrack in one scene. In 1983, producer Crile was "indefinitely suspended" from CBS for violating the network's news guidelines.

10. LOVE, SIDNEY (NBC), 1981

Tony Randall starred as Sidney Shorr, a lonely, middle-aged homosexual who sets up housekeeping with an unwed mother and her young daughter. The series was based on a popular 1978 made-for-TV movie. In the movie, Sidney's homosexuality had been treated matter-of-factly: it was soft-pedaled, but not avoided. By the time the series went on the air, conservative and religious groups had launched a major campaign against the show; they condemned it for "glorifying" homosexuality, promiscuity, and illegitimacy, and despite Tony Randall's public assertions that he would not allow the network to compromise his character's integrity, few traces of Sidney's homosexuality remained.

In response to angry accusations that NBC had caved in to homophobic pressure, the network's entertainment division president, Brandon Tartikoff, asserted that the Sidney character was still a homosexual, but that NBC simply had "no plans of bringing it up, dealing with it or mentioning it." To boost the series' erratic ratings once it aired, NBC juggled the show around in three different time slots. It was finally dropped from the schedule in 1983.

11. CONSENTING ADULT (ABC), 1985

In an ABC made-for-TV movie, Marlo Thomas and Martin Sheen portrayed parents trying to cope with the revelation that their nineteen-year-old son, played by Barry Tubb, is gay. Based on Laura Z. Hobson's 1975 novel (which independent producers had been trying to make into a movie for years), the film went further than previous television programs in its depiction of intimacy between gay men. It was particularly provocative, for network television, in a scene where the son tells his mother in reasonably explicit terms what he loves about men. The program was praised by straight critics in the mainstream press, but

Aidan Quinn, Gena Rowlands, Sylvia Sidney, and Ben Gazzara in NBC's drama about AIDS, *An Early Frost*.

received mixed reviews from gay critics, some of whom accused it of being bland and cautious.

12. AN EARLY FROST (NBC), 1985

Originally proposed in early 1983, this NBC made-for-TV movie, about a young gay lawyer with AIDS who confronts his family with his homosexuality and his illness at the same time, went through more than fourteen rewrites (three is the norm) before reaching the nation's TV screens. It was the first full-length, made-for-television film to deal with AIDS. In contrast to *That Certain Summer* thirteen years earlier, it not only provided the network's most realistic portrayal of a lover relationship between two gay men (Aidan Quinn and D.W. Moffett), but also contained television's first sympathetic characterization of a "radical queen" (John Glover), a character in the film who is dying of AIDS.

Despite early reports that NBC had censored the script to remove anything that might appear to condone homosexuality, the program received outstanding reviews in both the straight and gay press. It was also one of the top-rated shows in the Nielsens for its week: almost fifty million Americans watched the film. To the surprise and pleasure of many, it drew an even bigger audience than ABC's *Monday Night Football,* which was in the same time slot.

5 PROMINENT ACTORS WHO TURNED DOWN THE ROLE OF ZACH, THE DOCTOR, IN "MAKING LOVE"

1. TOM BERENGER
2. MICHAEL DOUGLAS
3. HARRISON FORD
4. WILLIAM HURT
5. PETER STRAUSS

NOTE: The film's director, Arthur Hiller, said that most actors, when approached about the role, flatly replied, "Don't even think about me for this." The part finally went to Michael Ontkean.

5 MOVIES THAT IN SOME WAY DEAL WITH HOMOSEXUALITY, AND WHAT THE MAINSTREAM CRITICS SAID ABOUT EACH

1. THE BOYS IN THE BAND (1970)

The film: Mart Crowley's play — the most famous of all plays about homosexuality — was first performed on the New York stage in April 1968. Crowley himself produced and wrote the screenplay for the 1970 film version. The film starred the original Off-Broadway cast, and was directed by William Friedkin, who later directed *The French Connection* and *The Exorcist.* The story is about a gathering of nine men — eight gay, one who insists he's not — at a birthday party, where, to varying degrees, they bare their souls.

What the critics said: *The Boys in the Band* broke new ground in tackling a formerly taboo subject on the screen — the private lives of homosexuals. But while theater critics had almost unanimously praised the stage play, the film received decidedly mixed reviews. Hollis Alpert, in *Saturday Review,* called it "an indulgence of truly extraordinary masochism, and one which all too neatly reveals the various hang-ups and self-hatreds of the participants in the party. Guilt eventually undoes [almost] everyone..."

Joseph Morgenstern, in *Newsweek,* labeled it "gross" and "irrevocably ungay." He wrote: "To convince us that homosexuals hate themselves, it generates so much self-hate that the movie itself turns hateful."

Critic George N. Boyd, writing in *The Christian Century,* praised the film for its tight construction, humor, and pathos, but noted, "The story might have been better balanced if at least one of the eight had advanced a cogent argument for the normalcy of homosexuality."

Pauline Kael wrote in *The New Yorker:* "William Friedkin brings out the worst of the play with guilt-ridden pauses and long see-the-suffering-in-the-face closeups. Every blink and lick of the lips has its rigidly scheduled meaning, and it's all so solemn — like Joan Crawford when she's thinking."

John Gruen in *Vogue* was one of the few critics to praise the film. He thought it was "explosive," "even better than the play," and called it "the best, most searing, and funniest look into the 'gay' life."

And critic Frank Rich, in *Time,* concluded: "If the situation of the homosexual is ever to be understood by the public, it will be because of the breakthrough made by this humane, moving picture."

Epilogue: Reacting to criticism from gays that the movie presented a distorted view of gay men as hostile and self-destructive and that it only reinforced conventional, negative stereotypes, Friedkin told one interviewer, "The film is not about homosexuality. It's about human problems. I hope there are happy homosexuals. There just don't happen to be any in my film."

2. DEATH IN VENICE (1971)

The film: Among the directors who had tried and failed over the years to bring Thomas Mann's novella *Death in Venice* to the screen were John Huston, Joseph Losey, and Jose Ferrer. It was Italian film director Luchino Visconti who finally succeeded, though not without difficulties. Mann's story — about a disillusioned, middle-aged artist who becomes obsessed with a beautiful fourteen-year-old boy during a vacation to Venice — scared off numerous producers, who refused to finance the project. One Italian producer was willing to back the movie, but only if Visconti turned the fourteen-year-old boy into a luscious adolescent nymphet a la Lolita. Finally, Warner Brothers, which had released Visconti's *The Damned* in 1969 (and had made money doing it), agreed to finance the film and gave Visconti a free hand in directing it.

What the critics said: After *Death in Venice* had its world premiere in London in 1971, the critics pounced, with vehemence and indignation. Visconti had made several changes from the novella. First and foremost, he had changed the book's central character, Aschenbach, from a writer to a composer. He had also added several flashback scenes, which awkwardly attempted to clarify Aschenbach's character. But perhaps most galling to some critics was that the homosexual implications of the story seemed more pointed in the film than they did in the book. The critics went on the defensive, often suggesting that the movie was some kind of sordid homosexual fantasy concocted by the "flamboyantly" homosexual Visconti.

Stefan Kanfer wrote in *Time:* "Mann's *Death in Venice* is, in fact, no more about homosexuality than Kafka's *The Metamorphosis* is about entomology . . . This film is worse than mediocre; it is corrupt and distorted . . . it is irredeemably, unforgivably gay."

Saturday Review's Hollis Alpert wrote: "To simply have Aschenbach turn queer, to have him pursue Tadzio as though in search of forbidden erotic pleasure, amounts to a gross distortion of Mann's meaning. Even more vulgar is the camera's fixation on the boy's buttocks, an implication that Aschenbach is a budding sodomite."

Paul D. Zimmerman in *Newsweek* disdainfully dismissed the film as "a requiem for an aging homosexual."

National Review's David Brudnoy called it "a high-fashion exploitation drag."

There were exceptions to the general indignation.

Penelope Gilliatt in *The New Yorker* described *Death in Venice* as a film "of unearthly beauty . . . It is plainly the work of a great man."

Rex Reed in *Holiday* concluded that it "is not a masterpiece without reservations, but it is a very compelling and distinguished piece of art."

And in the London Sunday *Times,* critic Dilys Powell wrote: "In the past quarter of a century there have been films potentially more influential . . . I can think of none which has been more truly a work of art."

Epilogue: Critical appreciation of Visconti's film has steadily increased since its premiere in 1971. It is now justifiably regarded by many as Visconti's masterpiece.

3. LA CAGE AUX FOLLES (1978)

The film: Directed by Edouard Molinaro, and written by Francis Veber, who later wrote the screenplay for the American comedy *Partners, La Cage aux Folles* was based on a long-running hit French stage play. For the movie, Ugo Tognazzi and Michel Serrault took the roles of two gay lovers, Renato and Albin, who own a fashionable Saint Tropez nightclub featuring female impersonators. Albin is the club's star performer. When Laurent, Renato's son from a long-ago heterosexual encounter, announces he is going to be married, the two lovers try to act straight for their meeting with the bride's austere, moralistic family. Albin, in drag, pretends to be Laurent's mother — with disastrous results. But there is a happy ending.

What the critics said: *La Cage aux Folles* caught most critics off-guard: it was a sleeper hit. Though the film opened in New

Zaza Albin (Michel Serrault), disguised as a woman, is greeted by the Secretary General of the Union for Moral Order (Michel Galabru), in *La Cage aux Folles*.

York in the spring of 1979, most critics paid little or no attention to it, and some of those who did didn't write reviews until as late as August.

Brendan Gill wrote in *The New Yorker:* "We laugh almost without stop at the increasingly frantic means by which Renato and Albin seek to transform themselves for Laurent's sake, but little by little something much more interesting than mere farce emerges from the slapstick somersaultings of the plot; we begin to find Albin and Renato affecting as well as amusing. For they have put their lives in jeopardy to please a boy and girl unworthy of them; the more chances they take, the more our hearts go out to them."

David Ansen wrote in *Newsweek:* "The clockwork formulas — and the image of homosexuals as swishy queens — are old-fashioned, but Tognazzi and Serrault manage to invest their parts with great comic zest and delicate pathos." The film, he said, was "laugh-out-loud funny."

Richard Schickel wrote in *Time:* "Though the gays must make eccentric adjustments to the exigencies of living, their behavior is viewed as no more unusual than the quirks everyone develops to get through the day as pleasantly as possible." He called the film "the warmest comedy of the year ... giddy, unpretentious, and entirely lovable."

Critic Robert Hatch, of *The Nation,* liked the film but had reservations about it: "*La Cage aux Folles* capitalizes on the kind of hysterical exhibitionism that serious-minded homosexuals repudiate. The film is funny enough, if you're not in the line of fire, but I'm not prepared to say that the fun is entirely harmless."

One of the only critics to pan it outright was Vincent Canby in the New York *Times.* "*La Cage aux Folles,*" he wrote, "is naughty in the way of comedies that pretend to be sophisticated but actually serve to reinforce the most popular conventions and most witless stereotypes." He condemned it as foolish and mechanical. "Even worse, though," he wrote, "is the awful sentimentality."

Epilogue: With grosses in excess of $40 million, *La Cage aux Folles* became the highest grossing foreign film of all time, a distinction it held until 1986. It was nominated for several Academy Awards, including for best director and best screenplay adapted from another medium, and spawned two sequels and a hit Broadway musical.

4. CRUISING (1980)

The film: Directed by William Friedkin, who had directed *The Boys in the Band* a decade earlier, *Cruising* was based on a 1970 Gerald Walker novel about a series of gruesome murders within New York's gay S&M community. Al Pacino played a heterosexual cop who immerses himself in gay life in order to bait and trap the killer. In the process of tracking the murderer, he becomes troubled about his own sexual identity. The movie had barely started location shooting on the streets of New York when it became the object of daily protests by gay activists, who insisted that, by focusing on the S&M scene, the film would foster distorted attitudes among straight people about gay life and would trigger anti-gay violence. To ease some of their concerns, Friedkin put a brief disclaimer at the beginning of the film suggesting that his depiction of New York's gay S&M community was not meant to be representative of the gay community as a whole. It was not enough. A single unsolved murder at the end of the film still left many viewers with the impression that Pacino himself had become a brutal killer simply after being exposed to gay life.

What the critics said: Critics were almost unanimous in their condemnation of the film.

William Friedkin's *Cruising*: "something to offend almost everyone."

Vincent Canby wrote in the New York *Times:* "Homosexual activist groups, which have been protesting the production of *Cruising* on the grounds that it would present a distorted view of homosexual life, were right. *Cruising* is a homosexual horror film."

Time magazine critic Frank Rich noted that "Cruising is not anti-gay any more than a film like *American Gigolo* is anti-heterosexual." He nonetheless described the film as "hopelessly fouled up . . . defeated by narrative loopholes, unconvincing plot twists . . . This detective drama has something to offend almost everyone."

David Ansen wrote in *Newsweek:* "What Friedkin's film is about is anybody's guess. If he just wanted to make a thriller, he has made a clumsy and unconvincing one. If he wanted to explore the psychology of his characters, he has left out most of the relevant information. If he intended to illuminate the tricky subject of S&M, he hasn't even scratched the surface." He dismissed much of the film as "a superficially shocking tableau for the titillation and horror of his audience."

Roger Angell, in *The New Yorker,* wrote: "The picture goes on to suggest that homosexuality is catching and inescapably brutal: if you hang around with gays and the leather set, you will end up dead or killing someone. No one is immune — not an upright, heterosexual cop, not a quiet, unaggressive homosexual bystander. Being gay is a dangerous business. This is a shocking conclusion for any movie to come to. . ."

Epilogue: Despite the protests and various calls for a boycott, *Cruising* grossed an impressive $5 million in its first five days of release. However, the grosses soon plummeted, and the movie eventually bombed. One major hitch in its distribution occurred when the largest theater chain in the country, the General Cinema Corporation, refused to honor its advance bookings of the film; the GMC claimed that because of the film's explicit scenes of sadomasochistic sex, *Cruising* should have been rated X instead of R and was therefore unsuitable for distribution to its theaters.

5. MAKING LOVE (1982)

The film: *Making Love* — the story of a young, married doctor who comes to realize he is gay and who leaves his devoted wife — was one of the first major Hollywood releases to try presenting a non-hysterical, reasonably positive view of gay life. It was directed by Arthur Hiller (who had directed *Love Story*), and was released on Valentine's Day 1982. The screenplay was by Barry Sandler, based on a story from A. Scott Berg. The film starred Michael Ontkean as the doctor, Kate Jackson as his wife, and Harry Hamlin as the gay novelist with whom the doctor has his first homosexual affair.

What the critics said: Most critics praised the film's good intentions while often deploring what they saw as its naive and simplistic characterizations and conclusions.

Richard Schickel wrote in *Time:* "The people who made this picture are not interested in tragedy or even human messiness. They are determined to prove not only that 'nice boys do,' but that homosexuals can be as well-adjusted and as middle class as anyone else."

Stanley Kauffmann wrote in *The New Republic:* "Care has been taken to sanitize the script. The troubled husband and wife are childless. The male lovers are a doctor and a novelist, and the job the doctor gets in New York is at the Sloan-Kettering Institute. (No one who's working to cure cancer can be all bad, can he, even if he's homosexual?)"

David Ansen wrote in *Newsweek:* "Like other 'pioneering' Hollywood movies about minorities (*Gentleman's Agreement, Guess Who's Coming to Dinner?*), the minority in question is presented in terms wholesome enough to win a Good Housekeeping Seal of Approval . . . Still, one must applaud the attempt to reverse sexual stereotypes, however banal the results."

Lindsy Van Gelder wrote in *Ms.*: "*Making Love* unquestionably represents a long-overdue Hollywood breakthrough — if only because it validates up to now invisible gay lives." However, she noted, "most of the movie isn't a whole lot deeper than *General Hospital.*"

Critic Judith Crist called it "simple-minded, soapy, and sappy," and Leonard Maltin dismissed it as "bland."

Janet Maslin, in the New York *Times,* described it as "a thoroughly old-fashioned, wonderfully sudsy romance," and wrote that much of it was "rip-roaring awful in an entirely enjoyable way."

Epilogue: *Making Love* grossed only $12 million at the box office.

43 NOTABLE ACTORS WHO HAVE APPEARED IN DRAG IN THE MOVIES

1. CHARLIE CHAPLIN (*The Masquerader,* 1914; *A Woman,* 1915)
2. LON CHANEY (*The Unholy Three,* 1925)
3. LIONEL BARRYMORE (*Devil Doll,* 1936)
4. JACK BENNY (*Charley's Aunt,* 1941)
5. MICKEY ROONEY (*Babes on Broadway,* 1941)
6. CARY GRANT (*I Was a Male War Bride,* 1949)
7. ALEC GUINESS (*Kind Hearts and Coronets,* 1950)
8. RAY BOLGER (*Where's Charley,* 1952)
9. TONY CURTIS (*Some Like It Hot,* 1959)
10. JACK LEMMON (*Some Like It Hot,* 1959)
11. PETER SELLERS (*The Mouse That Roared,* 1959)
12. BING CROSBY (*High Time,* 1960)
13. ANTHONY PERKINS (*Psycho,* 1960)
14. DANNY KAYE (*On the Double,* 1961)

15. JACK GILFORD (*A Funny Thing Happened on the Way to the Forum,* 1966)
16. PHIL SILVERS (*A Funny Thing Happened on the Way to the Forum,* 1966)
17. LEE J. COBB (*In Like Flint,* 1967)
18. DUDLEY MOORE (*Bedazzled,* 1967)
19. RAY WALSTON (*Caprice,* 1967)
20. CHRISTOPHER HEWETT (*The Producers,* 1968)
21. HELMUT BERGER (*The Damned,* 1969)
22. YUL BRYNNER (*The Magic Christian,* 1970)
23. GEORGE SANDERS (*The Kremlin Letter,* 1970)
24. JOEL GREY (*Cabaret,* 1972)
25. LOU JACOBI (*Everything You Always Wanted to Know About Sex, But Were Afraid to Ask,* 1972)
26. JEFF BRIDGES (*Thunderbolt and Lightfoot,* 1974)
27. TIM CURRY (*The Rocky Horror Picture Show,* 1975)
28. MARLON BRANDO (*The Missouri Breaks,* 1976)
29. ROMAN POLANSKI (*The Tenant,* 1976)
30. MICHEL SERRAULT (*La Cage aux Folles,* 1978; *La Cage aux Folles II,* 1980; *La Cage aux Folles III,* 1986)
31. MICHAEL CAINE (*Dressed to Kill,* 1980)
32. GEORGE HAMILTON (*Zorro, The Gay Blade,* 1981)
33. RUTGER HAUER (*Chanel Solitaire,* 1981)
34. ROBERT VAUGHN (*S.O.B.*, 1981)
35. JOHN LITHGOW (*The World According to Garp,* 1982)
36. STEVE MARTIN (*Dead Men Don't Wear Plaid,* 1982)
37. ROBERT PRESTON (*Victor/Victoria,* 1982)
38. DUSTIN HOFFMAN (*Tootsie,* 1983)
39. TED McGINLEY (*Revenge of the Nerds,* 1984)
40. GENE SIMMONS (*Never Too Young To Die,* 1985)
41. RICHARD PRYOR (*Jo Jo Dancer, Your Life Is Calling,* 1986)
42. DOM DELUISE (*Haunted Honeymoon,* 1986)
43. JOHN CANDY (*Armed and Dangerous,* 1986)

36 HOT ACTORS WHO SHUCKED THEIR CLOTHES FOR THE CAMERAS, AND IN WHAT MOVIES YOU CAN SEE THEM NAKED

1. ALAN BATES
   King of Hearts (1966) and *Women in Love* (1970)
2. JEFF BRIDGES
   Rancho Deluxe (1975), *Winter Kills* (1979), and *Starman* (1984)
3. KEITH CARRADINE
   Nashville (1975)
4. NICHOLAS CLAY
   Excalibur (1981) and *Lady Chatterley's Lover* (1981)
5. FREDERICK COMBS
   The Boys in the Band (1970)
6. RICHARD GERE
   American Gigolo (1980) and *Breathless* (1983)
7. MEL GIBSON
   Gallipoli (1981) and *Lethal Weapon* (1987)
8. STEVE GUTTENBERG
   The Bedroom Window (1987)
9. ED HARRIS
   Knightriders (1981)
10. JOHN HEARD
    Cat People (1982)
11. DUSTIN HOFFMAN
    Marathon Man (1976)
12. WILLIAM HURT
    Altered States (1980) and *Body Heat* (1981)
13. DON JOHNSON
    The Magic Garden of Stanley Sweetheart (1970)
14. CHRISTOPHER JONES
    Three in the Attic (1968)

Mel Gibson. People went to see *Lethal Weapon* just for the ten-second nude scene.

15. BURT LANCASTER
    The Swimmer (1968)
16. JOHN LAUGHLIN
    Crimes of Passion (1984)
17. BRUNO LAWRENCE
    Smash Palace (1981)
18. ROB LOWE
    Youngblood (1986)
19. MALCOLM McDOWELL
    Caligula (1980) and *Britannia Hospital* (1982)
20. RUDOLF NUREYEV
    Valentino (1977)
21. RYAN O'NEAL
    Partners (1982)
22. AL PACINO
    Scarecrow (1973) and *Cruising* (1980)

23. JAMESON PARKER
The Bell Jar (1979)

24. MANDY PATINKIN
Yentl (1983)

25. SEAN PENN
Bad Boys (1983)

26. WILLIAM PETERSEN
To Live and Die in L.A. (1985)

27. DENNIS QUAID
The Night the Lights Went Out in Georgia (1981)

28. STEVE RAILSBACK
Lifeforce (1985)

29. OLIVER REED
Women in Love (1970)

30. ARNOLD SCHWARZENEGGER
The Terminator (1984)

31. SYLVESTER STALLONE
Party at Kitty and Studs (1970) (a.k.a. *The Italian Stallion*)

32. STING
Brimstone and Treacle (1982)

33. ROBERT URICH
Endangered Species (1982)

34. JAN-MICHAEL VINCENT
Buster and Billie (1974)

35. CRAIG WASSON
Ghost Story (1981)

36. TREAT WILLIAMS
Hair (1979)

9 ON-SCREEN MOUTH-TO-MOUTH KISSES BETWEEN MEN

1. Raf Vallone and Jean Sorel: *A View from the Bridge* (1962)
2. Kirk Douglas and Alex Cord: *The Brotherhood* (1968)
3. Rod Steiger and John Phillip Law: *The Sergeant* (1968)
4. Michael York and Anthony Corlan: *Something for Everyone* (1970)
5. Peter Finch and Murray Head: *Sunday, Bloody Sunday* (1971)
6. Al Pacino and John Cazale: *The Godfather, Part II* (1974)
7. Alan Bates and George de la Pena: *Nijinsky* (1980)
8. Michael Ontkean and Harry Hamlin: *Making Love* (1982)
9. Christopher Reeve and Michael Caine: *Deathtrap* (1982)

FROM SAPPHO TO THE JOY OF GAY SEX: 15 OUTRAGEOUS ACTS OF CENSORSHIP IN THE HISTORY OF GAY PEOPLE

"Censorship of anything, at any time, in any place, on whatever pretense, has always been and always will be the last cowardly resort of the boob and the bigot."

— Eugene O'Neill

1. SAPPHO'S LOVE POEMS

The greatest love poet of the ancient world, Sappho (610-580 B.C.) wrote hundreds of poems celebrating both homosexual and heterosexual love, and was esteemed by the ancient Greeks as "The Tenth Muse." Unfortunately, several hundred years later, Christian zealots did not agree. In A.D. 380, her books were ordered burned by St. Gregory of Nazianzus, who dismissed her as "a lewd nymphomaniac." In 1073, what little of her work survived was subjected to another purge, by decree of Pope Gregory VII: Sappho's poetry was publicly burned by ecclesiastical authorities in both Constantinople and Rome. By the twelfth century, all that remained of Sappho's writing were two complete poems and a handful of fragments. In 1897, archaeologists working in Egypt discovered numerous ancient coffins lined with papier-mached scraps of papyrus scrolls, which turned out to be shredded fragments of Sappho's poetry. Similar scraps were also found wadded into the carcasses of mummified crocodiles and other animals at the same site. It is only because of this discovery that we have as much of her work as we do today, still only a scant five percent of the original body of her writing — seven hundred lines out of the estimated twelve thousand that she actually penned.

2. MALE NUDES IN THE SISTINE CHAPEL

The powerful male nudes of Michelangelo's *The Last Judgment* scandalized much of Counter Reformation Italy, and even the gay poet and pornographer Pietro Aretino expressed horror at the sight of so much nudity in the Sistine Chapel, the Pope's private place of worship. In 1559, five years before Michelangelo's death, the Vatican hired artist Daniele de Volterra to paint loincloths on the more explicit male nudes in the fresco, forever earning Volterra the mocking title *il Brachettone* — "the Breeches Maker." After the Council of Trent's rigid decrees on decency in 1563, *The Last Judgment* was actually threatened with complete destruction for a time. Only the protests of various Italian artists and noblemen saved the fresco from being completely whitewashed by zealous moralists.

3. MICHELANGELO'S LOVE SONNETS

Michelangelo's genius was expressed not only as a painter and sculptor, but as a poet as well, and in 1623, fifty-nine years after his death, a volume of his impassioned love sonnets, most of them originally addressed to men, was published for the first time. Because of the explicitly homoerotic nature of many of the poems, the editor of the volume, Michelangelo's great-nephew, changed masculine pronouns to the feminine, deleted many of the more graphic homosexual references, and then bogusly claimed that all of the poems had actually been inspired by Vittoria Colonna, a devoutly religious, sixty-year-old widow with whom Michelangelo had had a close friendship. It was not until almost 350 years later, in 1960, that a completely restored, definitive edition of the poems was finally published.

4. THE WELL OF LONELINESS

A hysterical review in a London Sunday newspaper prompted English authorities to ban Radclyffe Hall's novel about lesbianism shortly after the book's publication in 1928. Critic James Douglas had written that he "would rather give a healthy boy or a healthy girl a phial of prussic acid than this novel" — a remark that immediately boosted the book's sales and sent vice authorities running to sweep up copies of it. At a public trial to decide whether or not the book was obscene, defense attorneys were forbidden from calling any of the forty literary critics they had assembled to testify on behalf of the novel. The presiding magistrate eventually ruled that the novel's literary merits — and he admitted it had many — actually worked against it, since the better written an obscene book was, the more corrupting was its influence. The book was judged obscene, and despite various appeals, not until twenty years later could it finally be published and sold in England. Meanwhile, in the United States, vice officers raided the office of the book's American publisher in 1929 and seized over eight hundred copies remaining from the sixth edition; they then staged a similar raid on Macy's book department. New York publisher Donald S. Friede was arrested and charged with circulating indecent literature. Like their English counterparts, American attorneys sought to defend the book on the grounds that it had literary merit; however, as in England, the court ruled that the testimony of literary experts was inadmissible. Despite the fact that the novel had been praised by Havelock Ellis, George Bernard Shaw, H.G. Wells, and others, the U.S. court finally ruled that "The book can have no moral value since it seeks to justify the right of a pervert to prey upon normal members of a community. . ." The judge further declared that although the book contained no obscene words or indecent phrases, its subject matter was "calculated to corrupt and debase." He ordered that it be banned. A few months later, however, a higher court overturned his decision, and *The Well of Loneliness* was finally cleared for sale in the U.S. Thanks in large part to all of the accusations of obscenity surrounding it, the novel eventually sold in excess of 100,000 copies.

5. THE LIFE OF HORATIO ALGER

American writer Horatio Alger (1834-1899) was best known for his "rags to riches" boys' novels, which were popular in the late nineteenth century. Alger himself was ardently homosexual, with a penchant for teenage boys; he was once run out of Brewster, Massachusetts for his sexual involvement with some of the local youths. Herbert Mayes' "definitive" biography of Alger, published in 1928, made no mention of Alger's homosexuality, but instead portrayed him as a fun-loving heterosexual with a taste for fast women. Mayes' biography was the standard reference work on Alger's life for over sixty years. However, in 1974, Mayes confessed that the entire biography had been a fabrication, that he had completely censored the true facts of Alger's life and had invented the existence of a Horatio Alger diary that the biography was supposedly based on.

6. THE LAST JUDGMENT, AGAIN

In 1933, Michelangelo's Sistine Chapel nudes were once again the center of controversy. In New York City, U.S. Customs agents seized and held a shipment of European art books containing reproductions of Michelangelo's *The Last Judgment.* An assistant collector of customs, who had never heard of Michelangelo, deemed the reproductions obscene. A few days later, a very embarrassed Treasury Department acknowledged the mistake and relinquished the books.

7. THE 1936 FILM VERSION OF THE CHILDREN'S HOUR

In 1936, Lillian Hellman's play about lesbianism, *The Children's Hour,* was brought to the screen by producer Samuel Goldwyn and director William Wyler. Retitled *These Three,* the play was substantially bowdlerized: all of its lesbian characters were changed to heterosexuals, and the central lesbian love interest was changed to a standard heterosexual love triangle. By authority of the Motion Picture Production Code (whose job it was to safeguard public morals), censors forbade the studio, and even film critics, from mentioning that the movie had been based on Hellman's play.

8. THE WORKS OF ANDRE GIDE

In 1935, a New York bookseller was arrested and charged with circulating indecent literature after he sold a copy of Gide's autobiography, *If It Die,* to an undercover police officer. The book recounted Gide's coming to terms with his homosexuality as a young man. Fortunately, Judge Nathan D. Perlman later ruled that although Gide had "unveiled the darker corners of his life," the autobiography "as a complete entity was not obscene." In 1952, five years after Gide had won the Nobel Prize for literature, all of his works were placed on the Catholic Index of Forbidden Books. They were considered dangerous to faith and morals. Ironically, all of his works had also recently been banned in the Soviet Union.

9. A STREETCAR NAMED DESIRE

In Tennessee Williams' play, Blanche du Bois's young husband — a boy who shot himself on the beach one night — was a homosexual. For the 1951 screen version, the Motion Picture Production Code dictated that the homosexuality be entirely eliminated: in the film, Blanche's husband suffers merely from "nervousness." The film's director, Elia Kazan, said, "I wouldn't put the homosexuality back in the picture if the code had been revised last night and it was now permissible. I don't want it. I prefer debility and weakness over any kind of suggestion of perversion."

10. ALLEN GINSBERG'S POETRY

In 1957, two officers of the San Francisco police department arrested poet and publisher Lawrence Ferlinghetti on charges of having published *Howl and Other Poems* by gay poet Allen Ginsberg. Police Captain William Hanrahan described the work as "obscene and filthy," and told reporters, "When I say filthy, I don't mean suggestive. I mean filthy words that are vulgar." After a lengthy trial and two weeks of deliberation, Judge Clayton Horn freed Ferlinghetti and ruled that Ginsberg's poetry was not obscene. Horn's written opinion, which is still regarded as a major codification of the obscenity law in California, pointed out: "Life is not encased in one formula whereby everyone acts the same or conforms to a particular pattern. No two persons think alike. We are all made from the same mould, but in different patterns. Would there be any freedom of press or speech if one must reduce his vocabulary to vapid innocuous euphemism? An author should be . . . allowed to express his thoughts and ideas in his own words."

11. THE "H" WORDS

In 1961, the Motion Picture Association of America relaxed its thirty-year code prohibiting the portrayal of homosexuality on America's movie screens. However, in 1962, the MPAA still

ABC disemboweled *Cabaret* for prime-time viewing.

refused to grant its Seal of Approval to Basil Dearden's film *Victim,* because it actually used the words "homosexual" and "homosexuality" on screen.

12. GAY PERSONALS ADS

In 1969, a well-known London underground newspaper, the *International Times,* began running personals ads for gay men alongside its usual personals for heterosexuals. The new section was called, simply, "Males." Police subsequently raided the newspaper's editorial offices and the paper's printers. The newspaper's three directors were charged with conspiring "to induce readers to resort to . . . homosexual practices and thereby to debauch and corrupt public morals." They were also charged with conspiring "to outrage public decency by inserting advertisements containing lewd, disgusting and offensive matter." All three men were found guilty. The House of Lords was asked to review the case and decided, by a four-to-one majority, that the newspaper's directors had been rightfully convicted of conspiring to corrupt public morals. But, perplexingly, they set aside the conviction for conspiring to outrage public decency — leading one wry commentator to note that what corrupts us does not apparently outrage us.

13. NEWSPAPER ADS FOR THE BOYS IN THE BAND

When William Friedkin's film version of *The Boys in the Band* opened across the country in 1970, major daily newspapers in Chicago, San Francisco, and Boston refused at first to carry ads for it. The ads showed actor Leonard Frey on the left side of the ad with the caption "Today is Harold's birthday"; on the right side was a picture of actor Robert La Tourneaux, portraying a hustler, with the caption "This is his present." Ads for the R-rated movie were also initially rejected by the *Los Angeles Times* and the *New York Daily News.*

14. CABARET ON PRIME TIME

When ABC first broadcast Bob Fosse's *Cabaret* on prime time in 1975, all references to homosexuality and bisexuality, including the crucial plot element of Brian's affair with Maximilian, were removed by network censors.

15. THE JOY OF GAY SEX

In 1979, British customs officials seized and burned five hundred copies of *The Joy of Gay Sex.* True to the neurotic nature of censorship, they ignored two hundred copies of *The Joy of Lesbian Sex* in the same shipment. However, in 1984, British customs officials seized and shredded copies of *both* books.

19 BOOKS RECENTLY BANNED, OR NEARLY BANNED, BECAUSE OF GAY OR LESBIAN THEMES

1. SAINT GENET, by Jean-Paul Sartre

In 1984, Sartre's biography of French writer Jean Genet was condemned as "indecent and obscene" by the British customs office, which seized and destroyed it.

2. THE FRONT RUNNER, by Patricia Nell Warren

Citizens of Three Rivers, Michigan, tried to have it removed from the shelves of the public library in 1982, because it "promotes homosexuality and perversion."

3. KADDISH AND OTHER POEMS, by Allen Ginsberg

In 1976, it was banned from high school English classes in Aurora, Colorado, on the grounds it was immoral.

4. IOLAUS: AN ANTHOLOGY OF FRIENDSHIP, by Edward Carpenter

A reprint edition of Carpenter's 1902 classic was seized and destroyed in 1984 by the British customs office, on the grounds it was "indecent and obscene." Ironically, when the book was first published in London more than eighty years earlier, it was not suppressed.

5. THE JOY OF GAY SEX, by Charles Silverstein and Edmund White

Copies were confiscated by local police from three Lexington, Kentucky, bookstores in 1977. In 1981, attempts were made to remove it from San Jose, California public libraries.

6. TELENY: A NOVEL ATTRIBUTED TO OSCAR WILDE

The nineteenth century classic of gay erotica, often attributed to Oscar Wilde, had been reprinted by an American publisher in 1983, and was seized and destroyed by British customs officials, who condemned it as "indecent and obscene."

7. DOG DAY AFTERNOON, by Patrick Mann

In 1978, officials at the Union High School Library in Vergennes, Vermont, removed the book to a special locked shelf. A 1980 court decision affirmed the school's right to keep the book locked away.

8. WHAT HAPPENED TO MR. FOSTER, by Gary W. Barger

Attempts to ban it from the Granville County, South Carolina, Public Library in 1982 were based on the fact that the novel's central character is a homosexual.

9. ONE FOR THE GODS, by Gordon Merrick

British customs officials seized and destroyed copies of it in 1984.

10. STEPPENWOLF, by Hermann Hesse

Although it is not in itself gay-themed, attempts to remove it in 1982 from the Glenwood Springs, Colorado, High School Library were due in part to the novel's references to lesbianism and so-called sexual perversion.

11. THE LORD IS MY SHEPHERD AND HE KNOWS I'M GAY, by Troy Perry

In 1982, the Niles, Michigan, Community Library considered removing it from the shelves because of its "pornographic" nature.

12. LET'S TALK HEALTH, by Kenneth L. Packer and Jeannine Bower

In Salem-Keizer, Oregon, attempts were made in 1986 to ban it from the local school district, because of the book's handling of such issues as masturbation and homosexuality.

13. SEXUAL DEVIANCE AND SEXUAL DEVIANTS, by Erich Goode and Richard Troiden

The St. Mary's, Pennsylvania, Public Library Board ordered it pulled from the shelves and destroyed in 1977.

14. SAPPHISTRY: THE BOOK OF LESBIAN SEXUALITY, by Pat Califia

It was seized and shredded by British customs in 1984. Attempts were made to delete it as a recommended text for college students at Long Beach State University in 1982. The book was felt to be "inappropriate."

15. THE YAGE LETTERS, by William S. Burroughs and Allen Ginsberg

It was banished in 1976 from high school English classes in Aurora, Colorado, on grounds of "immorality."

16. THE GAY REPORT, by Carla Jay and Allen Young

In 1982, there were attempts to ban it from the Niles, Michigan Community Library.

17. A WAY OF LOVE, A WAY OF LIFE, by Frances Hanckel and John Cunningham

In 1984, attempts were made to remove it from the library shelves of the Fairbanks, Alaska, North Star Borough School District. There were complaints that the book taught students "how to become queer dope users."

18. UNDERSTANDING GAY RELATIVES AND FRIENDS, by Clinton R. Jones

Citizens of Elkhart, Indiana, wanted it banned from the local public library in 1982. They claimed the book tried to "get people to accept the homosexual lifestyle, like there is nothing wrong with it."

19. RYDER, by Djuna Barnes

Was seized in 1984 by the British customs office on the grounds it was "indecent and obscene."

SOURCE: Robert P. Doyle. *Banned Books Week '86: A Resource Book.* Chicago: American Library Association, 1986.

3 SUPPRESSED MANUSCRIPTS OF FAMOUS GAY MEN

1. *MAURICE* BY E.M. FORSTER

The author of such English classics as *A Passage to India* and *A Room With a View* kept his most revealing manuscript under lock and key. *Maurice,* a novel about homosexual love, was begun by Forster in 1913, after an encounter with English social reformer Edward Carpenter and his lover, George Merrill. It was finished the following year. Forster believed that the novel's happy ending would prevent the book from being published in his lifetime. "If it ended unhappily," he wrote, "with a lad dangling from a noose or with a suicide pact, all would be well . . . But the lovers get away unpunished and consequently recommend crime." After Forster's death in 1970, all of his unpublished works, including *Maurice,* went to King's College, Cambridge. *Maurice* was finally published in 1971, to critical acclaim.

2. THE MEMOIRS OF HERMAN BANG

Bang was one of Denmark's leading nineteenth-century novelists and poets. After his death in 1912, there were rumors that he had left behind some memoir in which he posthumously revealed his homosexuality. Magnus Hirschfeld's Scientific Humanitarian Committee, an early gay rights group in Germany, urged the publication of the manuscript: "It is to be hoped that Herman Bang, who had an enthusiastic interest for our movement, spoke out even more clearly about the emotional side of his life in some manuscript that he may have left behind and that will hopefully not be withheld from the public." Unfortunately, Bang's literary executor and publisher, Peter Nansen, claimed that the work would bring "monstrous harm to Bang's name," and decided to suppress it.

3. THE MEMOIRS OF JOHN ADDINGTON SYMONDS

For eighteen months, from 1889 to 1890, English essayist and historian John Addington Symonds poured his energies into writing his memoirs, in which he candidly discussed his homosexuality and the personal torment of coming to terms with it. Symonds was anxious that the work be published — he thought it would be useful to later psychologists and researchers — but not until "a period when it will not be injurious to my family." When Symonds died in 1893, the work fell into the hands of his literary executor, Horatio Brown. When Brown died in 1926, he in turn bequeathed it to the London Library, with specific instructions that it not be published for fifty years. From 1926 to 1949, the work languished, unopened. The first person to ask permission to read it was Symonds' own daughter, Dame Katharine Furse, in 1949; but it wasn't until 1954 that the Library finally provided public access to the memoirs, and even then, because of its subject matter, only to "bona fide scholars." It wasn't until 1984 — almost one hundred years after it was written — that the manuscript was finally published.

5 "DIRTY" GAY NOVELS WRITTEN BEFORE 1930

1. THE SINS OF THE CITIES OF THE PLAIN; OR THE RECOLLECTIONS OF A MARY-ANNE (1881)

Written more than a decade before Oscar Wilde was sentenced to prison for lewd conduct with various young men and street hustlers, *The Sins of the Cities of the Plain* recounts the adventures of a successful male prostitute, Jack Saul, working the streets of late nineteenth-century London. Based on fact, it revealed a widespread, steamy side of Victorian society, and includes, among other episodes, the explicit confessions of a young soldier in the Foot Guards — "There are lots of houses in London where only soldiers are received, and where gentlemen can sleep with them" — and a description of a transvestite ball at a fashionable London hotel. "I believe the people of the house thought we were gay ladies," one of the characters remarks after leaving the ball. The book concludes that, "The extent to which pederasty is carried on in London between gentlemen and young fellows is little dreamed of by the outside public." Although it was less than a hundred pages long, and expensively priced at four guineas a volume, the book apparently sold very well.

2. TELENY, OR THE REVERSE OF THE MEDAL: A PHYSIOLOGICAL ROMANCE OF TODAY (1893)

Often attributed to Oscar Wilde, who probably only helped edit it, *Teleny* describes a passionate and tragic love affair between two men: the handsome young pianist Rene Teleny, and one of his adoring fans, Camille Des Grieux. Considered the most prominent example of nineteenth-century gay erotica, the book is florid in style and operatic in tone: people scream for mercy during sex, faint in the throes of orgasm, and more often than not an aroused penis is described in terms more appropriate to the launching of a battleship; it's the kind of book where people are not merely charismatic, but rather "*diabolically* charismatic." Almost every sexual encounter, gay or straight, has an unhappy outcome: a young maid kills herself after a sexual affair with a man; a handsome Arab has a bottle accidentally broken up his rectum during an orgy; and Des Grieux himself makes two unsuccessful suicide attempts, largely because he cannot cope with his "unnatural" desires. Perhaps fittingly, in the book's final, lurid chapter, Teleny himself commits suicide, after he prostitutes himself for some badly needed cash to Des Grieux's beautiful and wealthy mother.

3. PEDERASTIE ACTIVE (1906)

The author of this short French classic identified himself to history only as Mr. P.D. Rast. Written in a light-hearted, often farcical style, the books tells the story of an older man who seduces one willing male virgin after another. "A virgin boy's jissom is incomparably delicious," the author explains. "Only you who have tasted it, you blessed mortals, can know it!" His list of conquests includes two beautiful young brothers, Albert and Philippe, who he enjoys together in one sitting, and a handsome soldier named Thomas. Describing his fling in bed with Thomas, the author muses, in a style typical of the entire narrative, "God! Was he lovable! Especially his huge plunger. Ah, reader, pity my poor little asshole, because this terrifying machine is going to burrow itself so deeply that its blond fur will caress my orifice!"

4. ERNEST (1910)

Privately published in a limited edition by its author, the German book collector Werner von Bleichroeder, *Ernest* is the story of a beautiful nephew sexually enslaved by his strong, good-looking uncle, Gernand. "You are going to get used to the idea that your nudity and every part of your body belong to me," Gernand tells the boy, "and perhaps to quite a few other people besides, if I so choose." Young Ernest — who is devoted to his muscular uncle — is subjected to mouth-fuckings, fierce spankings, piss baths, and lessons in masturbation and fellatio, and is admonished that he is to become the willing sexual plaything of his classmates at school, or of any man who wants him. "These are the first lessons in the art of satisfying a man with your mouth," Gernand explains to the boy. "That will be henceforth your main job . . . Your face and mouth are made for it, and countless members will come to enjoy themselves in your little mouth, big ones and small ones, young ones and old ones, fat ones and skinny ones. And you will suck them all, till the hot stream of their passion is appeased by pouring down your throat!" In the final pages of the book, Ernest is forced into prostitution at a bar belonging to a well-hung ex-sailor, a friend of Gernand.

5. THE WHITE PAPER (1928)

"I have always loved the stronger sex," remarks the narrator of *The White Paper* at the start of the book. "As long as I can remember, and even looking back to that age when the senses have still to come under the influence of the mind, I find traces of the love I have always had for boys." Usually attributed to Jean Cocteau, *The White Paper* describes an adolescent boy's growing passion for classmates, sailors, and other working-class boys in the French port city of Toulon. Although the book contained a preface and several erotic illustrations by Cocteau, he never publicly acknowledged its authorship; however, it is widely regarded as "the most signatured of unsigned works." In one of the book's most memorable early episodes, the narrator develops a blinding crush on a virile, well-developed classmate at school; trying to declare his love to the boy, he makes a complete fool of himself instead. The boy, who charms everyone around him, later dies of pneumonia after an ill-advised swim in the Seine. In another scene, the narrator goes to a public bath where the proprietor has installed transparent mirrors so that he and his friends can watch men bathing: "Young members of the working class provided the show . . . Standing in the tub, they would gaze at their reflection (at me) pensively and start with a Parisian grin which exposes the gums. Next, they'd scratch a shoulder, pick up the soap and handling it slowly, make it bubble into a lather. Then they'd soap themselves. The soaping would gradually turn into caressing. All of a sudden their eyes would wander out of this world, their heads would tilt back and their bodies would spit like furious animals." The book ends with the narrator — wounded by the world's lack of acceptance of his sexuality — exiling himself from society.

2 UNFINISHED GAY NOVELS BY FAMOUS WRITERS

1. THE NOVEL OF AN INVERT by EMILE ZOLA (c. 1885)

Zola's novels were frequently condemned as pornography by conservative readers, and he often did his best to fan the flames of controversy, partly because he enjoyed the attention and partly because controversy helped to boost sales of his books. His celebrated novel about prostitution, *Nana* (which included references to lesbianism), was denounced as "gutter-sweeping" by some readers, and another, *La Terre,* was prosecuted in court by a member of the British Parliament who believed "nothing more diabolical has ever been written by the pen of man." But even the great French writer, for all of his disdain of middle-class morality, was worried about writing a novel about homosexuality. In the 1880s, as part of his twenty-volume *Natural and Social History of a Family under the Second Empire,* he started work on a novel called, simply, *The Novel of an Invert.* However, he finally abandoned it because he was afraid to publish it. His views on homosexuality sometimes seemed to contradict one another. He once wrote that "An invert is a disorganizer of family, of the nation, of humanity." On the other hand, he was also one of a handful of famous European literary figures who publicly backed Magnus Hirschfeld's international campaign to repeal stiffly anti-homosexual laws in Germany around the turn of the century.

2. FLOWERS OF ASPHALT by STEPHEN CRANE (1894)

Crane was already widely known for his novel about female prostitution, *Maggie,* when he decided, after being approached by a young male hustler in New York City, to write a novel about homosexuality, tentatively titled *Flowers of Asphalt.* On an April

Courtesy Public Library, Newark, New Jersey

Stephen Crane's unfinished novel about male prostitution, *Flowers of Asphalt,* horrified his close friend, author and critic Hamlin Garland. The manuscript has never been found.

night in 1894, Crane and a friend had been walking down Broadway when they were approached by what they at first thought was a young beggar but which turned out to be a male prostitute soliciting them. Intrigued, Crane invited the boy home, fed him, listened to his stories, and then gave him fifty dollars. Almost immediately, Crane started work on *Flowers of Asphalt,* about a boy who flees the country for New York City and becomes a prostitute. Parts of the manuscript were warmly praised by some of Crane's friends, but he apparently abandoned work on it after he read portions of it to author Hamlin Garland. Garland begged him to stop wasting his time and talent on such horrifying material. The unfinished manuscript has never been found.

12 COUNTRIES AND WHEN EACH DECRIMINALIZED HOMOSEXUAL ACTS BETWEEN CONSENTING ADULTS

1. FRANCE	1810
2. U.S.S.R.	1917 *
3. POLAND	1932
4. DENMARK	1933
5. SWITZERLAND	1942
6. GREAT BRITAIN	1967
7. EAST GERMANY	1968
8. WEST GERMANY	1969
9. NORWAY	1972
10. YUGOSLAVIA	1977
11. SPAIN	1980
12. NEW ZEALAND	1986

* Recriminalized 1934

22 COUNTRIES IN WHICH HOMOSEXUALITY IS STILL SPECIFICALLY PROSCRIBED BY LAW

1. ALGERIA
2. AUSTRALIA
3. CHILE
4. CHINA
5. CUBA
6. EGYPT
7. INDIA
8. IRAN
9. IRELAND
10. ISRAEL
11. LIBYA
12. MEXICO
13. MOROCCO
14. MOZAMBIQUE
15. NIGERIA
16. PAKISTAN
17. RUMANIA
18. SOUTH AFRICA
19. TANZANIA
20. TUNISIA
21. U.S.S.R
22. URUGUAY

5 GOVERNMENTS THAT HAVE ROUTINELY IMPRISONED, TORTURED OR EXECUTED GAY MEN

1. RUMANIA

Rumanian gays are routinely subjected to surveillance, arrest, beatings, official blackmail, and imprisonment. Shock therapy and castration are sometimes used by the government to "normalize" homosexuals. Once arrested, some gay men simply disappear without a trace. The Communist party rules the country with an iron hand, and gays are not the only targets of the government's repressiveness. Article 28 of the Rumanian constitution guarantees freedom of speech, assembly, meetings, demonstrations, and the press. However, Article 29 effectively reneges on these freedoms by prohibiting their use for any but state-approved, Communist causes. Homosexuals, like political, religious, and labor dissidents, face a variety of forms of repression, including forced psychiatric internment. Rumania is the only Eastern Bloc country in which homosexuality is still specifically proscribed by law.

2. IRAN

Iran's revolutionary government has routinely executed hundreds of homosexuals since it first seized power in 1979. Khomeini's reasoning towards the killings has been: "If your finger suffers from gangrene, what do you do? Do you let the whole hand, and then the body, become filled with gangrene, or do you cut the finger off?" The country's Islamic militia, the Pasdaran, uses beatings, torture, and blackmail against suspected homosexuals. However, many members of the Pasdaran are themselves reportedly homosexual and hold orgies using attractive young men who have been picked up on the streets and arrested on false charges.

3. CUBA

Until 1969, Castro's regime routinely incarcerated gay men in labor camps, where prisoners were subjected to deprivation, beatings, torture, and, in some cases, rape and castration. Although the camps were finally disbanded, homosexuals continue to be mistreated, arrested, and imprisoned under official government policies. The Committee for the Defense of the Revolution employs domestic spying to ferret out suspected homosexuals, as well as other non-comformists, including so-called "free-thinkers" and sexually liberated women. Gay men and lesbians are barred from membership in the Cuban Communist Party, and are regularly denied employment. Young people accused of being homosexual are often dismissed from the state-run university system, and a person seen simply holding hands with someone of the same gender can be put in jail for at least one year. Among the 125,000 people who fled Cuba in the Mariel boatlift were numerous gay men.

4. U.S.S.R.

Homosexual acts were legalized in the Soviet Union shortly after the Bolshevik Revolution. However, in 1934, Stalin made them illegal again, punishable by imprisonment for up to eight years. There were mass arrests of homosexuals; some were sent to prison or the labor camps, others were exiled or executed. Today, both gay men and those merely regarded by the KGB as "potential homosexuals" are subject to bureaucratic harassment, arrest, blackmail, beatings, torture, and imprisonment in the gulags. Article 121 of the Soviet criminal code prohibits a person from merely *being* a homosexual, whether one acts on the feelings or not. Within the labor camps, guards and other inmates are encouraged by administrators to harass and brutalize homosexual prisoners. Some homosexuals have reportedly been forced to undergo surgery in which sections of the buttocks are removed so as to disfigure the body and thus discourage any further homosexual activity. Like other dissidents and "undesirables," gays are also subject to forced hospitalization and psychiatric experimentation. Secretary Gorbachev's much-discussed policy of *glasnost* — "openness" — does not apparently extend to homosexuals: a Soviet newspaper article in the spring of 1987 called for the police to redouble their efforts in tracking down all homosexuals and halting homosexual activity.

5. CHILE

The right-wing military government of General Augusto Pinochet routinely employs torture against all forms of dissidents and "undesirables," including homosexuals. Documented cases of torture involve floggings, rape, beatings with metal rods and rubber hoses, electric shock, and burning with cigarettes and acids. Gay men, like other Chileans, are subject to random arrest, and have sometimes disappeared without a trace.

24 STATES IN WHICH HOMOSEXUAL ACTS BETWEEN CONSENTING ADULTS ARE STILL A CRIME

(As of May 1987)

1. ALABAMA
2. ARIZONA
3. ARKANSAS
4. FLORIDA
5. GEORGIA
6. IDAHO
7. KANSAS
8. KENTUCKY
9. LOUISIANA
10. MARYLAND
11. MICHIGAN
12. MINNESOTA
13. MISSISSIPPI
14. MISSOURI
15. MONTANA
16. NEVADA
17. NORTH CAROLINA
18. OKLAHOMA
19. RHODE ISLAND
20. SOUTH CAROLINA
21. TENNESSEE
22. TEXAS
23. UTAH
24. VIRGINIA

. . . plus the District of Columbia

THE 5 STATES WITH THE HARSHEST CRIMINAL PENALTIES FOR HOMOSEXUAL SODOMY

1. RHODE ISLAND
   Seven to twenty years in prison

2. MICHIGAN
   Fifteen-year maximum prison sentence for anal sex; five-year maximum prison sentence for oral sex

3. GEORGIA
   Twenty-year maximum prison sentence

4. IDAHO
   Five-year minimum prison sentence

5. TENNESSEE
   Fifteen-year maximum prison sentence

24 FAMOUS MEN WHO WERE ARRESTED ON GAY SEX OR MORALS CHARGES

1. JACQUES DE MOLAY (1243-1314), last grand master of the Knights Templar
2. SANDRO BOTTICELLI (1445-1510), Italian painter
3. LEONARDO DA VINCI (1452-1519), Italian painter and inventor
4. NICHOLAS UDALL (1505-1556), English playwright
5. MARC ANTOINE MURET (1526-1586), French writer
6. ANTHONY BACON (1558-1601), brother of Sir Francis Bacon
7. JEROME DUQUESNOY (1602-1654), Flemish sculptor

8. SAMUEL FOOTE (1720-1777), English actor and playwright
9. SIMEON SOLOMON (1840-1905), English painter
10. OSCAR WILDE (1854-1900), Irish playwright and wit
11. BILL TILDEN (1893-1953), U.S. tennis champion
12. HENRY COWELL (1897-1965), U.S. composer
13. WILLIAM HAINES (1900-1973), U.S. film actor
14. JEAN GENET (1910-1986), French writer
15. SIR JOHN GIELGUD (b. 1904), British actor
16. ALAN TURING (1912-1954), English mathematician and computer science pioneer
17. WALTER W. JENKINS (1918-1985), White House aide to President Johnson
18. MONTGOMERY CLIFT (1920-1966), U.S. actor
19. G. HAROLD CARSWELL (b. 1920), U.S. Supreme Court nominee
20. PIER PAOLO PASOLINI (1922-1975), Italian film director
21. JIM JONES (1931-1978), U.S. cult leader
22. ROBERT BAUMAN (b. 1937), former U.S. Congressman (R-Md.)
23. DANIEL CURZON (b. 1939), U.S. writer
24. JON HINSON (b. 1942), former U.S. Congressman (R-Miss.)

THE STORIES BEHIND 11 OF THOSE ARRESTS

1. JACQUES DE MOLAY (1243-1314), last grand master of the Knights Templar

The Knights Templar were a powerful religious-military order established at the time of the Crusades. Fear of their influence, and a desire for their wealth, prompted Philip IV of France to have them arrested *en masse* in 1308. They were charged with having committed sodomy and heresy. It was said that during initiation into the order new members were forced to kiss the anuses of their superiors and submit to homosexual intercourse. De Molay, grand master of the Templars, denied the charges of sodomy, but eventually confessed, under torture, to having committed heresy. He was burned at the stake.

2. LEONARDO DA VINCI (1452-1519), Italian painter and inventor

Leonardo was twenty-four when he was arrested on charges of having had sex with a seventeen-year-old male prostitute. He was given a conditional discharge, but two months later the charges were renewed, and he was arrested again. He spent a short time in jail, but was soon released, probably as a result of the intervention of highly-placed friends.

3. NICHOLAS UDALL (1505-1556), English playwright

Though best remembered today as the author of the first known English stage comedy, *Ralph Roister Doister,* Udall acquired a reputation of a different sort as a headmaster at Eton: he was overly fond of caning handsome young students. In 1541, he was imprisoned for having sex with two of his students and a servant. His incarceration lasted only a few months: his reputation as a playwright apparently helped him gain an early parole.

4. SIMEON SOLOMON (1840-1905), English painter

Described by John Addington Symonds as "a distempered and radically vicious soul," Solomon was a prolific artist whose work was obsessively erotic and often explicitly homosexual in theme. Among his admirers were Algernon Swinburne and Oscar Wilde. In 1873, when he was only thirty-three, he was arrested for soliciting sex in a public lavatory in London. When he was found guilty, his friends and patrons deserted him. He ended his life, some thirty years later, as a pavement artist, drawing sketches on the sidewalk and begging money from passersby.

5. ALAN TURING (1912-1954), English mathematician and computer science pioneer

A burglary at Turing's home led police to the discovery of a sexual involvement between the mathematician and a nineteen-year-old boy; Turing was arrested and charged with six counts of "gross indecency." Because of his international standing as a scientist, the court sentenced him to probation, but with the stipulation that he undergo medical treatment for his homosexuality. The treatment consisted of a series of female hormone injections to eliminate his libido — in other words, chemical castration. The injections left him impotent and caused him to grow feminine breasts; they also impaired his thinking. Barely two years after the arrest, and only a year after completing the court-ordered therapy, he committed suicide by eating an apple dipped in cyanide.

6. WALTER W. JENKINS (1918-1985), White House aide to President Johnson

A longtime aide and close personal friend of Lyndon Johnson, Jenkins was forced to resign from his post as Special Assistant to the President after he was arrested in 1964 on charges of having committed homosexual acts in a Washington D.C. YMCA, two blocks from the White House. He had been arrested once before, in 1959, on the same charges at the same YMCA.

7. MONTGOMERY CLIFT (1920-1966), U.S. actor

Shortly after Clift was nominated for an Academy Award for his performance in Fred Zinnemann's *The Search,* he was arrested for soliciting a young hustler on 42nd Street. His lawyers kept the incident hushed up.

8. G. HAROLD CARSWELL (b. 1920), U.S. Supreme Court nominee

Carswell was arrested in 1976 after allegedly soliciting a plainclothes police officer outside a shopping mall men's room in Tallahassee, Florida. In 1970, Carswell had been nominated to the Supreme Court by Richard Nixon; his nomination was rejected by the Senate because, among other things, he was regarded as an advocate of racial segregation. After his arrest in Florida, Carswell checked into a local psychiatric hospital. The restroom where he was arrested became a popular local tourist attraction, and eventually had to be closed.

9. JIM JONES (1931-1978), U.S. cult leader

Jones was arrested in 1973 for soliciting an undercover police officer at a gay porno theater in Los Angeles. The charges were later dropped. In 1978, he gained worldwide notoriety after engineering the mass murder-suicide of 913 of his followers at the so-called People's Temple in Guyana.

10. ROBERT BAUMAN (b. 1937), former U.S. Congressman

Bauman was arrested in 1980 for soliciting sex with a sixteen-year-old boy. "I have been plagued by two afflictions," he told the press, "alcoholism and homosexual tendencies. But I do not consider myself a homosexual." As a conservative Republican from Maryland, Bauman had consistently voted against gay rights issues in the House of Representatives, and was a vocal supporter of the Moral Majority. After his arrest, he made repeated assertions that he was being cured of his "homosexual tendencies"; in August 1983, however, he finally came out and admitted he was gay. His wife of twenty-one years immediately had their marriage annulled. He has since gone into private practice as a lawyer, and in 1986 he wrote *The Gentleman from Maryland: The Conscience of a Gay Conservative,* a personal memoir in which he spoke of the need for legal changes to protect gay men and lesbians from discrimination and harassment.

11. JON HINSON (b. 1942), former U.S. Congressman

Hinson, a Republican Representative from Mississippi, was arrested in 1976 for committing an obscene act at the Iwo Jima Memorial in Arlington, Virginia. In 1981, he was arrested again, this time in a House of Representatives men's room, and was charged with "oral sodomy" with a 28-year-old man. Hinson resigned from office shortly after his second arrest.

17 FAMOUS PEOPLE WHO SUPPORTED THE IDEA OF HOMOSEXUAL RIGHTS BEFORE 1930

1. MARTIN BUBER (1878-1965), Jewish religious philosopher
2. SIR RICHARD BURTON (1821-1890), English explorer and author
3. ALBERT EINSTEIN (1879-1955), German-U.S. physicist
4. HAVELOCK ELLIS (1859-1939), English sexologist
5. SIGMUND FREUD (1856-1939), Austrian founder of psychoanalysis
6. EMMA GOLDMAN (1869-1940), U.S. political activist
7. HERMANN HESSE (1877-1962), German novelist
8. KARL JASPERS (1883-1969), German philosopher
9. RICHARD VON KRAFFT-EBING (1840-1902), German neuropsychiatrist
10. THOMAS MANN (1875-1955), German author
11. RAINER MARIA RILKE (1875-1926), German poet
12. BERTRAND RUSSELL (1872-1970), English philosopher
13. MARGARET SANGER (1885-1960), founder U.S. birth control movement
14. GEORGE BERNARD SHAW (1856-1950), British playwright
15. LEO TOLSTOY (1828-1910), Russian author
16. H.G. WELLS (1866-1946), English author
17. EMILE ZOLA (1840-1902), French author

43 CELEBRITIES WHO HAVE OPENLY SUPPORTED GAY RIGHTS

1. EDWARD ASNER
2. PATTY DUKE ASTIN
3. LAUREN BACALL
4. JOAN BAEZ
5. RONA BARRETT
6. ROBERT BLAKE
7. RONEE BLAKLEY
8. CAROL BURNETT
9. CHIP CARTER
10. RICHARD COHEN
11. SIMONE DE BEAUVOIR
12. PHIL DONAHUE
13. MIKE FARRELL
14. HENRY FONDA
15. JANE FONDA
16. SIR JOHN GIELGUD
17. GUNTER GRASS
18. HUGH HEFNER
19. GRACE JONES
20. CORETTA SCOTT KING
21. CHRISTOPHER LEE
22. SHIRLEY MACLAINE
23. MARSHA MASON
24. ETHEL MERMAN
25. BETTE MIDLER
26. PAUL NEWMAN
27. OLIVIA NEWTON-JOHN
28. RICHARD PRYOR

29. MARTHA RAYE
30. LYNN REDGRAVE
31. VANESSA REDGRAVE
32. MAUREEN REAGAN
33. BURT REYNOLDS
34. JOAN RIVERS
35. JEAN-PAUL SARTRE
36. NEIL SIMON
37. GLORIA STEINEM
38. ELIZABETH TAYLOR
39. MARLO THOMAS
40. LILY TOMLIN
41. ABIGAIL VAN BUREN
42. NANCY WALKER
43. DENNIS WEAVER

15 CELEBRITY HOMOPHOBES

1. KEN KESEY (b. 1935), U.S. writer

In a 1986 interview in *Esquire* magazine, the author of *One Flew Over the Cuckoo's Nest* said that the homosexuals he knew were neither happy nor proud, and speculated that AIDS might be caused not by a virus but simply by homosexual acts themselves. "It seems to me," he remarked, "it's one's job to put sperm in a place that's designed for it." Referring to homosexuals in general, he said, "I'll bet you water in hell that when we tally up our beans at the end of the game, our good beans and our bad beans, that I've got more good beans than they do. I mean, why not go down the road that gives the most good beans?"

2. JACK LaLANNE (b. 1914), U.S. physical culturist

Incensed at the growing visibility of gay men in Los Angeles, the former king of television exercise announced in 1979 that he planned to march down a one-mile stretch of Sunset Boulevard with a 350-pound barbell on his shoulders in order to protest the "damn queers and homos and little boy prostitutes" who had "taken over Hollywood." LaLanne was forced to cancel the march after he was injured in a car accident.

3. AYN RAND (1905-1982), U.S. writer

She supported the repeal of laws prohibiting homosexual acts among consenting adults, but qualified that support with the conviction that homosexuality was "utterly disgusting." Her own brother-in-law, to whom she was very close, was gay.

4 HEDDA HOPPER (1890-1966), U.S. gossip columnist

Although she befriended numerous gay men in her private life, Hopper publicly railed against homosexuality and "faggots," as she called them, and often equated society's growing sexual permissiveness with the rise of Communism. A staunch Republican, she once hinted that Noel Coward and Democratic presidential candidate Adlai Stevenson were having an affair, and in 1963, she was sued by Elizabeth Taylor's second husband, Michael Wilding, for suggesting that he and Stewart Granger were lovers. (Hopper and her publisher settled out of court.) She felt it was her duty to expose homosexual activities within the film industry, even though her own manager was a well-known lesbian.

5. ELVIS PRESLEY (1935-1977), U.S. performing artist

Although he often paid lesbians to perform sexually for him, the self-described "king of the bad-asses" feared and detested gay men.

6. LITTLE RICHARD (b. 1935), U.S. performing artist

The manic rock performer who wrote "Tutti Frutti" and "Good Golly, Miss Molly" once described himself as a "flaming homosexual from Macon, Georgia." However after becoming a born-again Christian, he did an abrupt about-face, and warned in a 1980 interview in the *Tuscaloosa News,* "If your brother's a homosexual, you must protect your little boy from him. Because homosexuals are sick. And lesbians are sick, too. What real woman would want another woman to touch her? She'd feel like something was crawling on her." He has also said: "If God can save me, an old homosexual, He can save anybody."

7. JOSEPH BOTTOMS (b.1954), U.S. actor

After portraying a gay football player in the NBC miniseries *Celebrity,* Bottoms told *Us* magazine: "I don't hate gays, but I believe they're awfully unfulfilled human beings. I really think homosexuality is a dead-end. It's self-adulation. It's masturbation . . . I feel sorry for them because they're unnatural."

8. JOHN WAYNE (1907-1979), U.S. actor

In a 1976 *Advocate* interview, Wayne told interviewer Steve Warren, "So I see no reason to jump with joy because somebody is a gay and I don't see any reason for waving a flag for all the wonderful things gays have done for the world . . . any more than you'd say, 'Oh boy, hooray for the tuberculosis victim!' It's abnormal to me."

9. ERNEST HEMINGWAY (1899-1961), U.S. writer

He admitted he had "certain prejudices against homosexuality." He also admitted that the whole subject bitterly depressed him. According to one of his long-time friends, matador Sidney Franklin, Hemingway once spotted a man he thought was gay walking on the other side of the street in a town in Spain. "Watch this," Hemingway told Franklin. He walked across the street, wordlessly punched the man in the face, and then, with a satisfied grin on his face, just as wordlessly rejoined Franklin. Hemingway rejected Gertrude Stein's advice that he should pity, not hate, homosexuals, and angrily told her she was "queer and liked only queers." After their friendship ended bitterly, Hemingway began publicly disparaging Stein as "a woman who isn't a woman."

10. DONNA SUMMER (b. 1948), U.S. singer

Although gay audiences were primarily responsible for her rise to stardom as the queen of disco, Summer began condemning homosexuality after she became a born-again Christian, and she used her live concerts as a pulpit from which to claim that AIDS had been sent by God to punish gay men. She said she loved homosexuals as people but hated their homosexual acts. "God's plan was for Adam and Eve," she often remarked, "not Adam and Steve."

11. IRVING STONE (b. 1903), U.S. writer

In 1961, Stone wrote a 664-page bestseller, *The Agony and the Ecstasy,* about the life of Michelangelo — without once discussing the sculptor's homosexuality. Twenty years later, when "Dear Abby" mentioned in passing in one of her columns that Michelangelo had been homosexual, Stone wrote her to deny the "charge" and "slander," as he put it, and told her there was not "a scintilla of evidence to support the accusation." Stone's assertions prompted a flood of flabbergasted and indignant rebuttals, from laymen and art historians alike. After publishing some of the rebuttals in her daily column, Abby concluded that, "Alas, perhaps Irving left a few stones unturned."

12. MORT SAHL (b. 1927), Canadian-U.S. talk show host

On a 1975 television panel discussion about feminism, Sahl called for the executions of "faggots" and "homos." He denounced gay people as "destructive . . . a negative social force." "They are the enemy!" he warned. The program, in which he also characterized the American Civil Liberties Union as "lawyers for faggots," drew fierce protests and prompted a sit-in demonstration at the Los Angeles T.V. station where it was taped.

13. JOAN COLLINS (b. 1933), English actress

Collins told *Playboy* magazine in 1984, "There's a moral laxity around. Herpes and AIDS have come as the great plagues to teach us all a lesson. It was fine to have sexual freedom, but it was abused. Apparently, the original AIDS sufferers were having 500 or 600 contacts a year, and they are now inflicting it on heterosexuals. That's bloody scary. It's like the Roman Empire. Wasn't everyone running around just covered in syphilis? And then it was destroyed by the volcano." After receiving widespread criticism for her remarks, she tempered some of her outspokenness. Asked about AIDS by *People* magazine one year later, she tersely replied, "Enough has been said about this issue by people who are not knowledgeable. It should be left to doctors and politicians to discuss, not actors."

14. EDDIE MURPHY (b. 1961), U.S. entertainer

Murphy aroused a storm of controversy when, on a 1983 HBO comedy special, he made jokes abouts AIDS and "faggots," and told the audience, "I'm afraid of gay people. Petrified. I have nightmares about gay people . . . Ladies be saying gay men are the best friends to have . . . You know what's real scary about that? That new AIDS shit . . . It petrifies me 'cause girls be hanging out with them. And one night they could be in the club having fun with their gay friend and give 'em a little kiss and go home with AIDS on their lips." When he was later asked in *Rolling Stone* magazine about the criticism his routine generated, Murphy replied, "I think homosexuals didn't get offended by this. Faggots who have nothing to fucking do but sit around with tight asses and feel like people are pointing fingers at them . . . people who are insecure got offended." His reaction to the Eddie Murphy's Disease Foundation — a group that took out ads in various national publications to protest his remarks — was that they could "Kiss my ass."

15. THE U.S. OLYMPIC COMMITTEE

In 1982, the United States Olympic Committee sued organizers of San Francisco's Gay Olympics claiming that the USOC had exclusive use of the word "olympics" and that the name Gay Olympics infringed on their copyright. They sought and received an injunction barring use of the name Gay Olympics. Gay organizers argued, unsuccessfully, that more than a dozen other "olympics" — including the Special Olympics, the Police Olympics, the Armenian Olympics, even the Rat Olympics and the Crab-Cooking Olympics — had gone on for years unchallenged by the USOC. Not only was the USOC's position upheld in court, but organizers of the Gay Olympics were eventually ordered to pay the Committee $96,000 in legal fees. The decision was appealed to the Supreme Court, which in June, 1987, ruled against the Gay Olympics, which are now known as, simply, the "Gay Games."

17 OUTSPOKEN ANTI-GAY POLITICIANS

1. GEORGE BUSH, U.S. vice president

During the 1980 Presidential campaign, Bush told reporters, "I don't think homosexuality is normal behavior, and I oppose the codification of gay rights." Bush repeated his opposition to gay rights while campaigning with Reagan for re-election in 1984. In 1986, Bush addressed a gathering of Moral Majority leader Jerry Falwell and his followers, and told them, "America is in crying need . . . of the moral vision that you have brought."

2. WILLIAM REHNQUIST, U.S. Supreme Court chief justice

Writing on the case of a gay campus organization seeking official recognition at a university, Rehnquist compared homosexuality to a communicable disease and said that the question was akin to whether people suffering from measles had a constitutional right to violate quarantine regulations and spread their disease among healthy individuals. Rehnquist also voted — along with Supreme Court Justices Byron White, Warren Burger, and Sandra Day O'Connor — to uphold an Oklahoma law prohibiting homosexuals or those defending or promoting a homosexual lifestyle from teaching in public schools. In 1986, he voted with the court's majority to uphold the constitutionality of Georgia's antisodomy laws.

3. PHIL GRAMM, U.S. Senator (R-Texas)

During the 1984 election campaign, Gramm attacked his Democratic opponent for having accepted a $604 contribution from a gay rights group; Gramm turned the contribution into one of the major issues of the campaign. He has opposed gay rights legislation and has said that gay people should be prevented from becoming schoolteachers or from working in areas of national defense. He is best known as one of the authors of the Gramm-Rudman Balanced Budget Amendment.

4. RONALD REAGAN, U.S. president

On the campaign trail in 1980, Reagan told one interviewer, "I oppose gay rights ordinances because they require employers to hire people solely on the basis of sexual preference." He also said that he was against state legislation decriminalizing sex acts between consenting adults because "in the eyes of the Lord" homosexuality is "an abomination." At other times, he has called homosexuality "a tragic illness" and "a neurosis." He has made numerous anti-gay appointments, including the nomination of William Rehnquist as Chief Justice of the Supreme Court and, within his administration, the appointment of ultraconservative, anti-gay columnist Patrick Buchanan to the post of White House director of communications.

5. WILLIAM DANNEMEYER, U.S. Representative (R-Calif.)

As a member of the House Subcommittee on Health and the Environment, Dannemeyer has introduced various controversial AIDS-related legislation, including one bill that would cut off federal revenue-sharing funds to cities that do not close gay bathhouses and another that would give legislative approval to the practice of banning children with AIDS or AIDS-Related Complex from public schools. Dannemeyer opposes gay rights and has said that he has "no intention of elevating sodomy to the level of a protected civil right. It's not gay; it's tragic. What these people do — male homosexuals — in the name of sexual freedom is a perversion and it should be described as such." In 1987, Dannemeyer co-sponsored a bill to require mandatory HIV-antibody testing for all U.S. residents.

6. JOHN GLENN, U.S. Senator (D-Ohio)

As a Democratic presidential hopeful in 1984, the former astronaut rebelled against the Democratic Party's platform because it included a gay rights plank. At a press conference, he told reporters he "doubted" whether homosexuals should be allowed to serve as soldiers, spies, YMCA directors, and schoolteachers. He opposed extending the 1964 Civil Rights Act to include gay people.

7. LYNDON LAROUCHE JR., three-time U.S. presidential candidate

LaRouche has blamed the AIDS crisis on the "dirty sexual habits" of homosexuals and on elected officials who "traded away their morals" by supporting gay rights. "A person with AIDS running around is like a person with a machine gun running around shooting up a neighborhood," he has said. He has advocated quarantining AIDS victims and people who test positive to the HIV virus. In an attempt to legally mandate LaRouche's views, his followers put a "Stop AIDS" initiative on the 1986 California ballot. Their slogan was "Spread panic, not AIDS." The initiative was defeated.

8. PATRICK J. BUCHANAN, conservative activist

A one-time Nixon speechwriter and former assistant to President Reagan, Buchanan has written that, in a healthy society, homosexuality "will be contained, segregated, controlled, and stigmatized, carrying both a legal and a social sanction." He has blamed homosexuality for the disintegration of the American family, and has said that "to disqualify a teacher on the grounds of professed homosexuality seems neither mean-spirited nor irrational." Contemplating the AIDS epidemic, Buchanan wrote,

"The poor homosexuals. They have declared war on nature, and now nature is exacting an awful retribution."

9. ELDRIDGE CLEAVER, U.S. writer and political activist

The former avowed Marxist and militant Black Panther became a born-again Christian in the late 1970s and then converted to Mormonism in 1983. In an interview in the *San Francisco Chronicle,* Cleaver called homosexuality "the work of Satan," and claimed that birth control proponents are led by "lesbian ideologues" who want to "thwart the male sperm in its sacred mission in sexual intercourse." He has also alleged that there is a "unisexual ideology that has been structured into our clothing and is being pushed by organized homosexuals." Cleaver has become active in Republican politics in California. In 1986, he made an unsuccessful bid for the U.S. Senate.

10. ROBERT K. DORNAN, U.S. Representative (R-Calif.)

"The biggest mass murderers in history are gay," Dornan once told the press; he has also stated that the majority of homosexuals are child molesters. A former TV producer and talk show host elected from California's deeply conservative 38th District (encompassing most of Orange County), he has vigorously opposed gay rights legislation of any kind.

11. JAMES GRIFFIN, Mayor of Buffalo, New York

Known for his fierce, often highly pejorative anti-gay rhetoric, Griffin publicly opposed one downtown gay bar's attempts to move into a larger building. "I'm against it," he told the *Buffalo News,* "and you can put that in the goddamn headlines. I don't use the term 'gay bars.' To me, they're not gays, they're fruits." Several months later, Griffin vetoed a gay rights ordinance that had been overwhelmingly approved by the Buffalo city council; he said the purpose of the ordinance was "undoubtedly to increase the public's acceptance of homosexual conduct as a normal way of life." The council overrode the mayor's veto by a vote of nine to two. Griffin is currently serving his third term.

12. GEORGE DEUKMEJIAN, Governor of California

In 1983, Deukmejian vetoed a bill that would have banned discrimination against gay people in private employment. He has given signals that he would veto any similar bills that come before him. In 1986, he vetoed a bill that would have banned discrimination against people with AIDS or AIDS-Related Complex. He also vetoed $20 million in AIDS-related funding from the state budget.

13. DON L. NICKLES, U.S. Senator (R-Oklahoma)

"I love the homosexual, but I hate his sin," said born-again Christian Don Nickles, shortly after his election to the U.S. Senate in 1980. "Let's not forget what happened to Sodom and Gomorrah." The former businessman has been a strong opponent of gay rights. In 1987, he introduced the first legislation in the Senate to impose mandatory testing for the HIV-antibody. Nickle's bill would require testing for anyone convicted on charges of prostitution, rape, or drug-related crimes. He was re-elected to another six-year term in 1986.

14. ROBERT BORK, U.S. Circuit Court of Appeals judge

In a 1984 court decision involving a 27-year-old petty officer discharged from the Navy for having engaged in homosexual acts, Bork ruled that homosexuals have no constitutional right to privacy. Bork, who previously served as U.S. Solicitor General under Richard Nixon and who implemented Nixon's infamous "Saturday Night Massacre" in 1973, supported the Navy's policy of automatically discharging homosexuals and wrote that while "activities relating to marriage, procreation, contraception, family relationships and child rearing and education" were protected by a constitutional right to privacy, homosexual conduct was not. He added that it was within the rights of the government to impose moral beliefs on the private lives of its citizens.

15. JESSE HELMS, U.S. Senator (R-North Carolina)

During Helms' 1984 re-election campaign, his television ads warned voters about the growing menace from "sexual deviates.' His campaign tried to discredit opponent James Hunt by publicly accusing him of having the support of "queer groups," and some of Helms' supporters went so far as to spread rumors that Hunt had once had a sixteen-year-old male lover. A former Sunday school teacher, and a favorite among religious fundamentalist groups, Helms strongly supported the defeated, anti-gay Family Protection Act in Congress, a bill that called for no "special" civil rights for gays and mandated that no homosexual could receive federal funds under such programs as Social Security, welfare, or veterans' and students' assistance. In 1986, Helms vigorously opposed a District of Columbia law forbidding insurance companies from using the HIV antibody test to deny people insurance coverage.

16. GARY POTTER, President of Catholics for Christian Political Action

As president of the influential conservative lobbying group Catholics for Christian Political Action, Potter helped organize support for the Family Protection Act, and has been quoted as saying, "There will be no satanic churches, no more free distribution of pornography, no more abortion on demand, no more talk of rights for homosexuals. When the Christian majority takes control, pluralism will be seen as evil and the state will not allow anybody the right to practice evil."

17. GARY JARMIN, political lobbyist for Christian conservatives

A powerful political consultant for fundamentalist Christian political groups, Jarmin sees homosexuality as "a threat to people's homes, families, and children. You send your kid to Sunday school where they teach him homosexuality is wrong, then on Monday they tell him in school gay is OK and the kid in the next seat has AIDS. It's a downward slide into the pit of immorality." Jarmin has asserted that the goal of Christian political activism is "political takeover from the grass roots up." He has received various letters of commendation from President Reagan, and was invited to both of Reagan's inaugurals.

59 U.S. CITIES AND COUNTIES THAT HAVE SOME FORM OF GAY RIGHTS PROTECTION

1. Alfred, New York
2. Amherst, Maine
3. Ann Arbor, Michigan
4. Aspen, Colorado
5. Atlanta, Georgia
6. Austin, Texas

7. Berkeley, California
8. Boston, Massachusetts
9. Buffalo, New York
10. Chapel Hill, North Carolina
11. Columbus, Ohio
12. Cupertino, California
13. Davis, California
14. Detroit, Michigan
15. East Lansing, Michigan
16. Evanston, Illinois
17. Harrisburg, Pennsylvani·
18. Hartford, Connecticutt
19. Honolulu, Hawaii
20. Iowa City, Iowa
21. Ithaca, New York
22. Laguna Beach, California
23. Los Angeles, California
24. Madison, Wisconsin
25. Malden, Massachusetts
26. Marshall, Minnesota
27. Milwaukee, Wisconsin
28. Minneapolis, Minnesota
29. Mountain View, California
30. New York City, New York
31. Oakland, California
32. Palo Alto, California
33. Philadelphia, Pennsylvania
34. Portland, Oregon
35. Pullman, Washington
36. Rochester, New York
37. Sacramento, California
38. Saginaw, Michigan
39. San Francisco, California
40. Santa Barbara, California
41. Seattle, Washington
42. Troy, New York

43. Tucson, Arizona
44. Washington D.C.
45. West Hollywood, California
46. Yellow Springs, Ohio
47. Clallam County, Washington
48. Dane County, Wisconsin
49. Hennepin County, Minnesota
50. Howard County, Maryland
51. Ingham County, Michigan
52. King County, Washington
53. Minnehana County, South Dakota
54. Montgomery County, Maryland
55. Multnomah County, Oregon
56. Northampton County, Pennsylvania
57. San Mateo County, California
58. Santa Barbara County, California
59. Santa Cruz County, California

9 CITIES WHERE GAY RIGHTS ORDINANCES WERE REPEALED BY VOTERS

1. Miami, Florida
2. San Jose, California
3. St. Paul, Minnesota
4. Wichita, Kansas
5. Eugene, Oregon
6. Davis, California*
7. Lincoln, Nebraska
8. Houston, Texas
9. Duluth, Minnesota

*Voters in Davis upheld a second gay rights ordinance in 1986, after repealing the first one in 1982.

15 U.S. CITIES THAT HAVE ELECTED OPENLY GAY CANDIDATES TO PUBLIC OFFICE

1. Ann Arbor, Michigan
2. Boston, Massachusetts
3. Brattleboro, Vermont
4. Bunceton, Missouri
5. Key West, Florida
6. Laguna Beach, California
7. Lunenburg, Massachusetts
8. Madison, Wisconsin
9. Minneapolis, Minnesota
10. Provincetown, Massachusetts
11. Rochester, New York
12. San Francisco, California
13. San Mateo, California
14. Santa Cruz, California
15. West Hollywood, California

9 PERFECTLY DISGUSTING REACTIONS TO AIDS

1. A LAW AGAINST TOUCHING

In 1985, Republican state legislators in Pennsylvania proposed a law which would have made it a first-degree misdemeanor for any person with AIDS to touch a non-infected person. The law specifically prohibited a person with AIDS from touching non-infected individuals on the breast, genitals, groin, inner thigh, buttocks or anus, even if the people were fully clothed. A repeat offense would have automatically elevated the charge to a felony. The bill died in committee.

2. A MURDER DEFENDANT WITH AIDS

A 1984 New York City murder trial became a national media event after it was learned that the defendant, Eddie Coaxum, had AIDS. Coaxum was accused in a drug-related stabbing death. Court officers showed up for the trial wearing protective surgical masks and rubber gloves. On the first day of jury selection, more than half of the 125 prospective jurors asked to be excused when they saw how the officers around them were garbed. According to *USA Today,* "Ten more walked out after Coaxum, 34, coughed several times." Despite assurances from New York City's health commissioner that AIDS could not be spread through the air or by casual contact, Coaxum himself was finally ordered to wear a mask and rubber gloves throughout the trial.

3. TO PRESERVE AND PROTECT

In August 1983, a Denver policeman, Officer Kevin Boyd, ran from a burglary victim's home after he learned that the man who had been burglarized had AIDS. Officer Boyd was taking a report from burglary victim Henry Pena, when Pena mentioned he had AIDS. "From the time I got up off the couch," Pena later said, "until I got to the door to explain he was in no danger, he was gone. He must've gotten in his police car and burned rubber." "Yes, I left in a hurry," Boyd later admitted; he told the press that Pena's $400 in missing jewelry "wasn't worth dying over."

4. THE HEALING PROFESSIONALS

In a nationally televised interview, a 27-year-old man with AIDS, Ken Ramsaur, told about lying in his hospital bed while two nurse's aides stood outside his door joking, "I wonder how long the faggot in 208 is gonna last." Ramsaur said they were "almost . . . placing bets." A 1984 study revealed that almost ten percent of the health care professionals at a large, urban hospital with several AIDS patients believed that "homosexuals who contract AIDS are getting what they deserve." A 1986 *MD Magazine* poll of 1500 physicians found that twenty-eight percent of the doctors favored some form of quarantine for people with AIDS. "We used to hate faggots on an emotional basis," an anonymous surgeon wrote the magazine. "Now we have a good reason."

5. DELTA AIRLINES

In 1985, Delta Airlines banned passengers with AIDS from flying on its aircraft. "The carrier will refuse to transport, or will remove at any point, any passenger . . . who is known to have acquired immune deficiency syndrome," the airline announced. A Delta spokesman claimed that people with AIDS posed a danger to other passengers, especially through the use of toilet seats and drinking cups. Delta rescinded the ban only after protests from numerous medical experts and gay rights groups. However, in 1986, a 31-year-old man with AIDS was forcibly removed from a Delta Airlines jet, allegedly because he was not accompanied by a medical attendant. Faced with adverse publicity and the threat of a nationwide boycott, Delta apologized for the incident.

In November 1986, another aspect of Delta's policies made front-page headlines. After 137 people were killed in the crash of a Delta jet at Dallas/Ft. Worth airport, lawyers for the airlines began making inquiries into one of the victim's homosexuality, in hopes of convincing a court that homosexuality, and the threat of AIDS to gay men, made the man's life worth less in terms of financial compensation to his family. The man's parents, who were suing Delta, successfully prevented the airlines' lawyers from mentioning their son's sexual orientation in court, and eventually won a $1 million settlement. A write-up of the case in *The Wall Street Journal* created a public furor, and Delta once again made a public apology.

6. CHRISTIAN CHARITY

In 1982, Jerry Falwell's Moral Majority began a campaign to lobby against federally funded research to find the cause of, and a cure for, AIDS. "If the medical community thinks that a new drug is what is needed to combat these diseases," said the Moral Majority's vice president, Cal Thomas, "it is deluding itself. There is a price to pay for immorality and immoral behavior." A 1983 Moral Majority newsletter read, in part: "Why should the taxpayers have to spend money to cure diseases that don't have to start in the first place? Let's help the drug users who want to be helped and the Haitian people. But let's let the homosexual community do its own research. Why should the American taxpayer have to bail out these perverted people?" Later, Falwell called homosexuality "sexual terrorism," and claimed that gay men "have expressed the attitude that 'they know they are going to die — and they are going to take as many people with them as they can.'" Equating civil rights for gays with the spread of AIDS, he urged followers to send him money to help in the fight against both. In 1984, a Stafford, Virginia group calling itself Christian Family Renewal mailed out fund-raising letters and a petition as part of its own campaign against AIDS. "You may soon fall victim to an irreversible, fatal disease!" warned the letters. "And it won't be your fault! But, you'll have to pay the terrible price anyway because of the promiscuous homosexuals, whose lustful lifestyles have created this uncontrollable incurable plague ... And now they've acquired their own distinct death-style, the AIDS plague, and like all their other rights, the homosexuals are forcing this painful, deadly disease on the rest of society ... Send the largest gift you can as if your life – and it very well may – depended on it. AIDS MUST BE STOPPED NOW!"

7. TELEVISION CREWS

In the summer of 1983, a television crew from the Manhattan ABC affiliate, WABC-TV, refused to enter the offices of Gay Men's Health Crisis Inc., an organization providing services to gay men with AIDS, to cover a story on the disease. Later, two backup crews also refused to enter the organization's offices. One of the technicians remarked, "Look, nobody knows anything about AIDS. What makes them so cocksure I'm not going to get it from a sweaty palm?" A similar incident occurred in a San Francisco television studio when two men with AIDS arrived to be interviewed on a local talk show. The studio crew refused to tape the segment and walked off the job. The two men were then relegated to a small makeup room, where they were interviewed by intercom. In March 1985, two men with AIDS were scheduled to appear on a local New York television program to discuss how various organizations were helping people with the disease. The WNBC television crew that was to have taped the segment walked off the set and refused to work near the men. A crewman was finally found who agreed to tape the segment, but only on the condition that the men put on their own microphones and then throw them away after the taping was over.

8. EXCOMMUNICATION

In 1986, a 26-year-old Ogden, Utah man dying from AIDS was excommunicated from his church after confessing his homosexuality to a local bishop. Clair Harward, a Mormon, had been told by doctors he had only a few months to live, when he went to his local Mormon bishop to confess and seek spiritual guidance. "I wanted peace of mind," Harward later explained. Instead, Mormon Bishop Bruce Don Bowen promptly excommunicated the dying man. Bowen further told Harward that he would be irresponsibly endangering public health if he continued to attend religious services. Harward died of AIDS-related complications shortly after the incident.

9. AND JUSTICE FOR ALL

In 1986, the U.S. Justice Department ruled that employers were within their legal right to fire employees who have AIDS, if the firing was based on fears, no matter how irrational, that the disease might be spread to other workers. The ruling was made despite overwhelming medical evidence that the disease cannot be spread through casual contact. Critics of the ruling immediately denounced it as "a disgrace . . . a sham . . . a license to discriminate." However, in 1987, the U.S. Supreme Court effectively reversed the ruling by including contagious diseases among the handicaps protected by federal anti-discrimination laws.

THE 12 U.S. CITIES WITH THE MOST CASES OF AIDS, AND WHAT PERCENTAGE OF THE NATIONAL TOTAL EACH CITY HAS

1. NEW YORK CITY	28.4%
2. SAN FRANCISCO	9.9
3. LOS ANGELES	7.1
4. HOUSTON	3.3
5. MIAMI	3.0
6. WASHINGTON D.C.	2.8
7. NEWARK, NEW JERSEY	2.4
8. CHICAGO	2.1
9. DALLAS	1.8
10. PHILADELPHIA	1.8
11. ATLANTA	1.6
12. BOSTON	1.5
Total	65.7%

SOURCE: Centers for Disease Control, March 1987.

25 PROMINENT PERSONS WHO HAVE DIED FROM AIDS

1. ROCK HUDSON, U.S. actor
2. LIBERACE, U.S. entertainer
3. ROY COHN, U.S. attorney
4. DAVE CONNORS, U.S. porno star
5. JERRY SMITH, U.S. football player
6. STEVEN STUCKER, U.S. actor
7. PERRY ELLIS, U.S. fashion designer
8. DIEGO RIVERA, U.S. human rights activist
9. TERRY DOLAN, U.S. conservative activist
10. PAUL KEENAN, U.S. actor
11. STEPHEN BARRY, former personal valet to Prince Charles
12. WAY BANDY, former make-up man for First Lady Nancy Reagan
13. NICHOLAS EDEN, Earl of Avon, son of former Prime Minister Anthony Eden and aide to Queen Elizabeth II
14. BERNARD "BUD" BROYHILL, U.S. human rights activist
15. ANTONIO LOPEZ, U.S. illustrator
16. WILLI SMITH, U.S. fashion designer
17. ROBERT LA TOURNEAUX, U.S. actor
18. DOUGLAS LAMBERT, British actor
19. STEWART McKINNEY, U.S. congressman (R-Conn.)
20. CHARLES LUDLAM, U.S. entertainer
21. REV. MICHAEL PETERSON, U.S. priest and physician
22. LYNNE CARTER, U.S. female impressionist
23. TOM WADDELL, U.S. decathlon athlete and gay rights activist
24. MICHAEL BENNETT, U.S. director and choreographer
25. J.W. KING, U.S. porno star

7 YEARS OF THE AIDS CRISIS, PRESIDENT REAGAN'S INITIAL BUDGET REQUEST FOR OVERALL SPENDING ON AIDS FOR EACH YEAR, AND WHAT CONGRESS WOUND UP ALLOCATING

	Reagan's Budget Request	**Research Funds**
1. 1981	-0-	-0-
2. 1982	-0-	$ 5.6 million
3. 1983	-0-	28.7 million
4. 1984	$ 39.8 million	61.5 million
5. 1985	60.5 million	109.2 million
6. 1986	126.0 million	233.8 million
7. 1987	203.4 million	410.7 million

SOURCES: Department of Health and Human Services. Office of Technology Assessment (U.S. Congress).

6 THINGS YOU CAN DO TO COMBAT AIDS

1. Use safe sex guidelines. Use condoms, avoid the exchange of body fluids, avoid activities such as rimming and fisting. Explore more the erotic potential of massage, creative masturbation, fetishes such as boots, underwear, blue jeans, leather. Activities that are presently considered unsafe include: anal intercourse without using a condom; oral sex carried to climax; sharing dildos and other sex toys; semen or urine in the mouth, anus, or open skin wounds; piercing; and "scat." Condoms should be used only with a water-soluble lubricant; remember, condoms are not foolproof and can fall off or tear.

2. Keep informed: about the disease, its symptoms and prevention; about revisions in safe sex guidelines; about updates in AIDS research. Also, know your potential sex partner. Talk before having sex.

3. Enjoy fewer partners more.

4. Avoid the use of recreational drugs.

5. Stay healthy. Eat right, get plenty of sleep, exercise regularly. Whether or not regular exercise and a good diet will help you avoid AIDS, they will at the very least help your body feel better and help you to feel better about yourself.

6. Become involved in the fight against AIDS. The more people involved in the fight against it, the fewer people it will eventually claim. Contribute, either with money or time, to research groups battling AIDS, to groups helping people who have the disease, to lobbying organizations fighting for more funding for AIDS research. Write letters to congressmen and others who have direct control over the amount of government money spent battling the disease. Remember: this is a disease that affects everyone. The money and time you spend today may one day directly benefit you, and will certainly benefit others.

12 TERRIBLE HISTORICAL EVENTS GAY PEOPLE HAVE BEEN BLAMED FOR

1. The destruction of Sodom and Gomorrah
2. The fall of the Roman Empire
3. Plague in Constantinople (A.D. 543)
4. The fall of Visigothic Spain to the Muslims
5. The decline of medieval Arabic civilization
6. The Black Plague
7. The decline of Renaissance Italy
8. The 1755 Lisbon earthquake
9. The rise of Nazi Germany
10. Earthquakes in California
11. The mid-1970s drought in the western U.S.
12. The appearance of AIDS

6 EARLY CHRISTIANS WHO HELPED SHAPE THE CHURCH'S ATTITUDES TOWARDS HOMOSEXUALS

"Virginity can be lost even by a thought."

— St. Jerome

1. PHILO JUDAEUS (20 B.C.-A.D. 50), Alexandrian philosopher

He claimed that homosexuality was on the increase in his own time, that homosexual practices led to sterility, and that homosexual men seduced and corrupted heterosexual men in order to spread "the disease of effemination." He believed that male homosexuality should be punished by death. His writings strongly influenced the development of early Christian ideology. For example, Philo was among the first Christians to expressly interpret the story of the destruction of Sodom and Gomorrah in homosexual terms. (Actually, the people of Sodom were probably destroyed for the sins of pride, adultery and inhospitality; the Bible makes no mention of homosexuality in connection with the story.) In other matters: Philo regarded the body as a prison and approved of circumcision because he thought it blunted a man's pleasure in intercourse. He often railed against women, since they were, in his opinion, the cause of man's fall in the Garden of Eden.

2. CLEMENT OF ALEXANDRIA (150-215), early Christian teacher and apologist

Born of non-Christian parents in Athens, he was converted to Christianity in his twenties while still a student. He has been called "one of the major intellectual leaders" of early Christianity. In his ethical and theological works, he condemned homosexuality, along with masturbation, oral sex, anal sex, and sexual pleasure for its own sake. Homosexuals, he preached, "stand self-condemned by their fine robe, their sandals, their bearing, their way of walking, the cut of their hair, and their glances." He approved of laws condemning them to the mines. He believed that semen was a human being in its most primal form and that to expend it in anything but procreational coitus was tantamount to murder.

3. ST. JOHN CHRYSOSTOM (347-407), Archbishop of Constantinople

He called homosexuality "the most severe of all plagues . . . a new and insufferable crime," and preached that homosexual acts were worse than murder. He urged parents not to let their sons wear long hair: long hair, he believed, was a sign of a corrupt spirit and made a boy more attractive to older men. Despite his horror of male homosexuality, he didn't think much of the alternative: he characterized women as "a necessary evil, a natural temptation, a desirable calamity, a domestic peril, a deadly fascination, a painted ill." He also wrote that lesbians were worse than male homosexuals, since women "ought to have more modesty." He condemned dancing, because it excited the emotions, and he denounced the theater, because he thought it taught people profanity, seduction, and intrigue. He is revered as one of the greatest teachers of the early Christian church.

4. ST. AUGUSTINE (354-430), Christian teacher and writer

Augustine apparently had at least one homosexual affair in his youth, and he was, by his own admission, tormented throughout much of his early life by an "insatiable" desire for sex. He converted to Christianity when he was thirty-three, after he read Paul's epistles. After that, he took a vow of celibacy, and concluded that the Church had every right to coerce people into unity with Christ. He preached that all non-procreational forms of sexuality — especially homosexuality — were grave sins, and that even procreational sex between husband and wife was inherently shameful, because it involved lust and continued the cycle of man's guilt that had begun with Adam and Eve. Celibacy, he preached, was the most blessed state: the world, he said, would be improved if all reproduction should cease.

5. JUSTINIAN (483-565), Byzantine emperor

He made homosexual acts punishable by torture, mutilation, and death. Punishment sometimes included amputation of the hands, if sacrilege had also been committed, but usually took the form of castration, in most cases involving amputation of both the penis and the testicles. Justinian and his wife, Theodora, a former prostitute who continued her legendary sexual activities under a guise of Christian piety, freely used the charge of homosexuality against personal and political enemies. In one instance, when a young man publicly insulted Theodora, she accused him of being a homosexual: she had him brutally tortured, and then had his penis lopped off so that he would bleed to death. Justinian blamed recent earthquakes, famine, and pestilence on homosexuals, who he claimed had provoked God's wrath.

6. ST. PETER DAMIAN (1007-1072), Christian reform leader

Orphaned at an early age and then brutalized by the older brother who raised him, Damian was tormented by sexual desire throughout his adolescence. To purge himself of carnal thoughts, he would immerse himself in ice water until his limbs were frozen and numb. As an adult, he ranted against the prevalence of homosexuality among the clergy, and begged the pope to take action against it. He characterized homosexuality as "the death of the body, the destruction of the soul," and claimed that even bestiality was preferable, since homosexuality involved the damnation of two souls, bestiality only one. He described the human body as "dirt" and "filth," and once wrote that a woman's labor pains were her just punishment for having engaged in intercourse.

HEAVENLY FATHERS: 6 GAY OR BISEXUAL POPES

1. POPE JOHN XII (937-964)

An insatiable bisexual, he was accused of running a brothel out of St. Peter's. He used the papal treasury to pay off his gambling debts, and enjoyed pranks such as ordaining a ten-year-old boy as bishop. Deposed once, he restored himself by force. He died, in his late twenties, after being badly beaten by a jealous husband.

2. POPE BENEDICT IX (1020-1055)

He turned the Lateran Palace into the site of lavish homosexual orgies, and by the time he was twenty-three his riotous conduct was so appalling that he was deposed. He was reinstated and deposed several times over the next five years. After finally being driven out once and for all in 1048, he died in obscurity. Some Catholic records, perhaps self-servingly, portray him as having died as a penitent in a monastery.

3. POPE PAUL II (1417-1471)

He wore a papal tiara that, according to one source, "outweighed a palace in its worth," and he plundered the papal treasury to satisfy his love of glitter and finery. Known to his cardinals as "Our Lady of Pity" for his tendency to cry at the slightest provocation, he allegedly died of a heart attack while being sodomized by one of his favorite boys.

4. POPE SIXTUS IV (1414-1484)

He took one of his beautiful young nephews, Pietro Riario, as his lover. Riario was charming and witty, and Sixtus made him a millionaire by plundering the papal treasury. Another young nephew, Girolamo, was also alleged to have been Sixtus's lover.

When Sixtus died, he left several million dollars in debts; but he is perhaps best remembered for consenting to the establishment of the Spanish Inquisition and for his appointment of Torquemada as its inquisitor-general.

5. POPE LEO X (1475-1521)

He acquired a reputation for being wildly extravagant. Among other things, he would play cards with his cardinals, allow the public to sit in as spectators, and toss huge handfuls of gold coins to the crowd whenever he won a hand. His expenses for both cultural and military endeavors, along with his taste for increasingly ornate papal gowns, drove the papal treasury into bankruptcy.

6. POPE JULIUS III (1487-1555)

He was lovers with both his bastard son, Bertuccino, and his adopted son, Innocente, and made the two of them cardinals. He also appointed numerous other handsome teenage boys as cardinals, and allegedly enjoyed bringing them together for orgies where he would watch them sodomize one another. Della Casa's famous poem "In Praise of Sodomy" was dedicated to him.

17 NOTEWORTHY FIRSTS

1. FIRST STATE TO DECRIMINALIZE HOMOSEXUAL ACTS

Illinois, in 1961.

2. FIRST SCIENTIFIC TREATISE ON HOMOSEXUALITY

A case history of two men passionately in love with members of their own sex was published in a German scientific journal, the *Magazine of Experimental Psychical Studies,* in 1791.

3. FIRST USE OF THE WORD "HOMOSEXUALITY"

The word "homosexuality" was coined by a Hungarian physician, Karoly Maria Benkert, in 1869, in an open letter to the Prussian minister of justice. The letter called for the repeal of laws persecuting homosexuals.

Early gay rights supporter Emma Goldman was labeled "the most dangerous woman in America" by the FBI.

4. FIRST MOVIE TO USE THE WORD "HOMOSEXUAL" ON SCREEN

Victim, in 1961. The film starred Dirk Bogarde as a gay lawyer who confronts a gang of blackmailers.

5. FIRST ENGLISH LAW CRIMINALIZING SODOMY

In 1553, Henry VIII made sodomy a felony punishable by death – the first law of its kind in English history. The statute remained in effect until 1967, although in 1861 the maximum penalty was changed to life imprisonment.

6. FIRST TRIAL OF OSCAR WILDE

Wilde was actually tried twice on charges of having committed acts of gross indecency. The first trial ended in a hung jury. Although he was given every opportunity and encouragement to jump bail and flee to Paris, he remained in England and was re-tried three weeks later. In the course of the second trial, he was found guilty and sentenced to two years hard labor.

7. FIRST USE OF THE WORD "HOMOPHOBIA"

The word "homophobia" was coined by author Wainwright Churchill in his 1967 book *Homosexual Behavior Among Males.*

8. FIRST OPENLY GAY U.S. JUDGE

Stephen M. Lachs was appointed to the Los Angeles Superior Court by California Governor Jerry Brown in 1979.

9. FIRST STATE TO PASS A STATEWIDE GAY RIGHTS BILL

Wisconsin, in 1981.

10. FIRST PUBLIC FIGURE TO OPENLY SUPPORT GAY RIGHTS IN THE U.S.

Political activist Emma Goldman, in the 1910s. In a 1923 essay written for Dr. Magnus Hirschfeld in Berlin, Goldman wrote: "I regard it as a tragedy that people of a differing sexual orientation find themselves proscribed in a world that has so little understanding for homosexuals and that displays such gross indifference for sexual gradations and variations and the great significance they have for living. It is completely foreign to me to wish to regard such people as less valuable, less moral, or incapable of noble sentiments and behavior." For this and other opinions, the FBI later dubbed her "the most dangerous woman in America."

11. FIRST OPENLY GAY CANDIDATE ELECTED TO PUBLIC OFFICE IN THE U.S.

Kathy Kozachenko, to the Ann Arbor, Michigan, city council in April, 1974. This first is often mistakenly credited to Elaine Noble, who was elected to the Massachusetts state legislature in November 1974.

12. FIRST GAY RIGHTS GROUP IN THE U.S.

The Chicago Society for Human Rights, founded in 1924.

13. FIRST USE OF THE WORD "HETEROSEXUAL"

The word "heterosexual" first appeared in the 1890s, in American medical journals. It originally referred to individuals sexually attracted to *both* sexes.

14. FIRST MODERN CONDOM

Invented by Italian anatomist Gabriello Fallopius in the

1500s. It was devised not as a contraceptive but as a protection against venereal disease. The first condoms were made of linen, then later of sheep gut or fish skin, and finally of rubber.

15. FIRST ENGLISH LANGUAGE PLAY TO DEAL WITH HOMOSEXUALITY

Christopher Marlowe's *Edward II,* in 1591.

16. FIRST MAINSTREAM MOTION PICTURE TO ACKNOWLEDGE NAZI PERSECUTION OF HOMOSEXUALS

Mel Brooks' *To Be or Not To Be,* in 1983. One of the main characters is a gay theatrical dresser forced to wear a pink triangle; he is later arrested and condemned to deportation to a concentration camp, but is saved at the last minute.

17. FIRST AND ONLY ALL-GAY ARMY

The Sacred Band of Thebes, composed entirely of 150 pairs of homosexual lovers who had taken a vow to stand or fall together. After many years unbeaten in battle, the Band was eventually annihilated by Alexander the Great's father, Philip II of Macedon, at the battle of Chaeronea in 338 B.C.

9 GAY TEACHERS

1. SOCRATES (469-399 B.C.)

Greek philosopher and teacher whose noble life and courageous death have made him one of the most admired figures in history. Socrates exploited the Athenian homosexual ethos as a basis of metaphysical doctrine and philosophical method.

2. PLATO (428-347 B.C.)

One of the most important thinkers and writers in the history of Western culture, Plato founded the Academy, an interdisciplinary school for research. Plato's teachings and writings take homosexual desire and homosexual love as the starting point from which to develop metaphysical theory.

3. BRUNETTO LATINI (1220-1295)

Florentine tutor of Dante. In *The Divine Comedy,* Dante praised his teacher for his "dear, kind and paternal countenance." Despite the accolades, Dante condemned Latini to the third round of the seventh circle of hell, a place reserved for sodomites.

4. GOLDSWORTHY DICKINSON (1862-1932)

English philosopher and lecturer at Kings College, Dickinson was a founder of the League of Nations. His 1896 masterpiece, *The Greek Way of Life,* as well as later writings on love between people of the same sex, gave indications that, as E.M. Forster later wrote, "all his deepest emotions were towards men."

5. LUDWIG WITTGENSTEIN (1889-1951)

Anglo-Austrian schoolmaster Wittgenstein's 1922 book *Tractatus Logico-Philosophicus* brought about a revolution in modern philosophy. Until recently, biographers have bent over backwards to avoid confronting his homosexuality and his long-term relationship with Francis Skinner.

6. F.O. MATTHIESSEN (1902-1950)

Harvard professor whose courses on American literature and the criticism of poetry made him the Ivy League's model of tutorial talent and commitment. The candid love letters between Matthiessen and his partner of twenty years, Russell Cheney, were recently published.

7. PAUL GOODMAN (1911-1972)

Lecturer, dissident, and author of *Growing Up Absurd,* Goodman claimed his homosexuality inspired his libertarian sense of humanity and a sense of beauty and democracy. But his unorthodox sexual behavior got him dismissed from a "progressive" boarding school.

8. WING BIDDLEBAUM (1919)

The smalltown schoolteacher in Sherwood Anderson's *Winesburg, Ohio* was much loved by the boys of his school. A "half-wit" became enamoured of him and in dreams imagined "unspeakable things" and went about telling them as fact. A mob ran Biddlebaum out of town. Anderson's story is the quintessential portrait of the homosexual teacher as victim.

Author Eric Rofes lost a job teaching near Boston after he came out publicly as a gay activist.

9. ERIC ROFES (b. 1954)

Rofes lost his sixth grade teaching job in the suburbs of Boston after coming out as a gay activist. He was later hired by an innovative private school where, with his students, he produced the best-selling *The Kids' Book of Divorce.* He tells about his years as a closeted gay schoolteacher in *Socrates, Plato & Guys Like Me: Confessions of a Gay Schoolteacher.*

11 EXAMPLES OF VICTORIAN PRUDERY AND IGNORANCE

1. "THE STOMACH DANCE"

When Oscar Wilde's play *Salome* was published in 1894, it contained several illustrations by artist Aubrey Beardsley, including one entitled "The Belly Dance." The book's publisher was so fearful that the word "belly" would offend readers that he changed the caption of the illustration to "The Stomach Dance."

2. PEDALING TO HELL

An 1867 medical journal article entitled "The Influence of the Sewing Machine on Female Health" claimed that seamstresses were apt to become sexually excited by the steady rhythm of a sewing machine's foot pedal, and that inadvertent orgasms often resulted from the up-and-down motion of women's legs while they were sewing. To prevent this, the article recommended putting bromide, which was thought to inhibit sexual desire, into the women's drinking water. It also suggested that supervisors circulate among the seamstresses to watch for anyone whose sewing machine was going too fast.

3. SEGREGATED BOOKSHELVES

One Victorian Era manual of decency and decorum, *Lady Gough's Book of Etiquette,* cautioned against placing books by female authors next to books by male authors on any bookshelf. The only exception was if the authors in question had been married in real life.

4. THE NAKED TRUTH

In 1858, British prime minister William Gladstone asserted that nudity had never been tolerated by the ancient Greeks, or by any other civilized society. He found the notion that nudity was acceptable to any cultivated society "incredible," and wrote "as it is not credible, so neither, I think, is it true."

5. THE WAGES OF SIN

An 1897 pamphlet on marital sex practices warned that fellatio causes cancer of the tongue.

6. CONTRACEPTIVES

In 1858, American birth control advocate Edward Bliss Foote was fined a total of $8000 for distributing an "obscene" pamphlet, *Words in Pearl for the Married,* which not only encouraged the use of contraceptives, but also advocated the right of women to decide when, or even whether, to have children.

7. A TERROR OF COCK

The word "cock" elicited such feelings of horror in some Victorian writers that for several decades much of the English language was rewritten to circumvent it. For example, the word "cockroaches" became simply "roaches." The "cock and bull story" became, among the more delicate minded, the "rooster and ox story." A cockswain was referred to as a "rooster swain." And a male turkey, instead of simply being referred to as a cock, was politely called "a gentleman turkey."

8. BOWDLERIZATIONS

Believing that the works of Shakespeare and other noted authors were not fit for family reading, Dr. Thomas Bowdler, a retired physician and a member of the "Society for the Suppression of Vice," published a ten-volume edition of Shakespeare in which all indelicate words, unsavory characters, and unwholesome acts were removed. The work was so successful with the general public that he went on to expurgate Gibbon's *The Rise and Fall of the Roman Empire,* from which he removed anything irreligious or immoral. Bowdler asserted that "If any word or expression is of such a nature that the first impression it excites is an impression of obscenity, that word ought not to be spoken nor written or printed; and, if printed, it ought to be erased." The verb "bowdlerize" — meaning "to expurgate, alter or emasculate" — was derived from his name.

9. THE LORD'S DAY

When Queen Victoria ascended to the throne in 1837, she issued a "Proclamation for the Encouragement of Piety and Virtue, and for the Preventing and Punishing of Vice, Profaneness, and Immorality." Among other things, it outlawed the playing of cards, dice, or any other game on Sunday, either in private or in public; it commanded people to attend church; and it outlawed the sale of alcoholic beverages on the Sabbath. Thus, the Victorian Era officially began.

10. CHICKEN PARTS

The words "leg" and "breast" were considered abhorrent in polite Victorian society, where they conjured up indecorous images of the human body. For years, frustrated doctors had to deal with censorious female patients who were unwilling to discuss exactly where an ailment was located. This loathing extended even to the dinner table, where people were instructed to request a "second wing" or "dark meat" when they wanted a chicken leg, or a "chicken bosom" when they wanted a breast.

11. INVISIBLE LESBIANS

When Queen Victoria was asked to sign the Criminal Law Amendment Act of 1885 – an act that originally provided only for the suppression of brothels, but which wound up including sweeping penalties for various forms of homosexual and lesbian conduct as well – she crossed out all references to lesbianism. Female homosexuals, she insisted, simply did not exist.

11 CONTEMPORARIES OF OSCAR WILDE AND WHAT EACH SAID ABOUT HIM

1. WALT WHITMAN, U.S. poet

During his 1882 tour of America, Wilde met Whitman at Whitman's home in Camden, New Jersey. Whitman later said of him: "I took him up to my den where we had a jolly good time. I was glad to have him with me, for his youthful health, enthusiasm, and buoyancy are refreshing. He was in his best mood and I imagine he laid aside any affectation he is said to have." Whitman found him "genuine, honest and manly." Wilde, for his part, left behind a 10-by-12 framed photograph of himself inscribed simply, "To Walt from Oscar."

2. JEFFERSON DAVIS, U.S. soldier and statesman

Davis's reaction to Wilde, after they met, at Wilde's insistence, in Mississippi in 1882, was characteristically terse. "I did not like the man," he said simply. Nonetheless, Wilde left Davis a framed, inscribed photograph of himself, just as he had with Whitman.

3. GEORGE BERNARD SHAW, British playwright

Long an admirer of Wilde's plays, he tried, after Wilde's imprisonment, to circulate a petition calling for the suspension of Wilde's sentence of two years hard labor. Only two other people were willing to sign it. In *My Memories of Oscar Wilde,* Shaw wrote: "Please let us hear no more of the tragedy of Oscar Wilde. Oscar was no tragedian. He was the superb comedian of his century,

U.S. writer Henry James. He called Oscar Wilde "an unclean beast." Pathetically, he spent much of his own life grappling with homosexual desires.

one to whom misfortune, disgrace, imprisonment were external and traumatic. His gaiety of soul was invulnerable."

4. HENRY JAMES, U.S. author

While George Bernard Shaw's petition was unsuccessfully making the rounds in London, a similar petition was being circulated by poet Stuart Merrill in the U.S. Among the people asked to sign it was novelist Henry James. He refused. James had met Wilde in Washington D.C. in 1882. Far from being charmed by Wilde's wit and drollery, James was repulsed by Wilde's flippancy. He wrote a friend: "Oscar Wilde is here — an unclean beast." At various other times, James referred to Wilde as "repulsive and fatuous," "a fatuous fool," and "a tenth-rate cad." He dismissed Wilde's plays as "cheap," "primitive," and "mechanical." Later, however, he did concede that Wilde's arrest and conviction were "hideously tragic," and that Wilde's imprisonment was "cruel." But still, he refused to sign a petition for Wilde's release.

5. JOHN ADDINGTON SYMONDS, English author and historian

Although he was himself homosexual, and although he and

Wilde had once had a brief, amiable correspondence, Symonds did not care for Wilde's effete form of homosexuality. "I resent the unhealthy, scented, mystic, congested touch which a man of this sort has on moral problems," he wrote a friend.

6. SIR ARTHUR CONAN DOYLE, English author

The creator of Sherlock Holmes met Wilde in London, at a dinner party arranged by a publisher. "It was a golden evening for me," Doyle later recalled. Wilde's conversation, he said, "left an indelible impression upon my mind. He towered above us all."

7. WILLIE WILDE, Oscar's brother

He once naively told George Bernard Shaw, "Oscar was not a man of bad character; you could trust him with a woman anywhere."

8. VISCOUNT CASTLEROSSE, English journalist

He became famous for his oft-quoted remark that Wilde was "every other inch a gentleman."

9. ANDRE GIDE, French author

Gide was twenty-one when he first met and, according to friends, fell in love with Wilde in Paris in 1891. They continued to see each other on and off during the next nine years, until Wilde's death in 1900. "There has been a great deal of folly written about Wilde," Gide wrote the year after Wilde's death. "Of course he was not 'a great writer.' A languid romancier, a bad poet, a good (but not superlatively good) dramatist — his works, taken without his life, present, to a sane criticism, a mediocre figure. But the man was consistent, extraordinary, vital even to excess, and his strange tragedy will always attract the consideration of the wise."

10. COLONEL GEORGE KEPPEL, English aristocrat

He summed up the feelings of much of Britain's aristocracy when, shortly after Wilde's death, he dismissed Wilde as "a frightful bounder," and remarked, "It made me puke to look at him."

11. LORD ALFRED DOUGLAS, Oscar's former lover

While testifying at a libel trial in 1918, eighteen years after Wilde's death, Douglas declared that Wilde "was the greatest force for evil that has appeared in Europe during the last 350 years." Douglas said he intensely regretted ever having met Wilde.

4 GAY VICTIMS OF THE NAZIS

1. COUNT ALBRECHT VON BERNSTORFF (d. 1945)

The nephew of the German ambassador to the U.S. during World War I, von Bernstorff was a retired Senior Counsellor at the German Foreign Ministry who used his personal and political connections to help Jews and other "undesirables" escape from the Nazi death machine. He was a member of the so-called Solf Circle, a group of aristocrats who opposed the oppression and savage persecution of human beings under the Nazi regime; they met regularly at the home of a Frau Anna Solf in Berlin. Von Bernstorff — monied, intelligent, middle-aged, and effetely homosexual — concentrated on getting Jews and other emigres safely out of the country with their belongings. He also used his diplomatic connections to warn the Dutch government of Hitler's planned invasion of Holland in 1940. Because of these activities, he has since been called "one of the most courageous opponents of Hitler." In the autumn of 1943, von Bernstorff and the rest of the Solf Circle were betrayed by a Swiss doctor who came regularly to the anti-Nazi salons; the man, Dr. Reckse, was actually an informant for the Gestapo. Reckse offered to carry letters from the anti-Hitler conspirators to their friends and fellow resisters in Switzerland. Instead, he took the incriminating letters directly to Heinrich Himmler, and on January 12, 1944, all of the Circle's members were arrested. Von Bernstorff was incarcerated in Lehrterstrasse prison in Berlin. His life was spared for over a year because Himmler thought he might eventually prove useful. However, on April 23, 1945, with the Russians at the edge of the German capital, von Bernstorff was taken outside with several other prisoners and lined up against a wall. An SS detachment, acting on Himmler's orders, mowed them down with machine guns.

2. "INGA" (d. 1943)

Posthumously awarded the Order of St. Olav, the highest civilian honor that the King of Norway can confer on a Norwegian subject, Inga was a female impersonator who worked for the Resistance after the Nazis occupied Norway in 1940. His family had disowned him when they discovered he was gay, and he went to Oslo looking for work as a female impersonator in one of the local cabarets. After 1940, he became involved in the Resistance and used his convincing impersonations to slip back and forth across the border to Sweden with information on Nazi shipping movements in the North Sea; a woman aroused less suspicion than a man. In the autumn of 1943, he was returning from Sweden when he was attacked by a group of drunk Nazi soldiers at the border. After trying to rape him, they discovered he was a man. He was arrested, brutally tortured, and then executed. A portrait of him, in full drag, hangs today in the Resistance Museum in Oslo.

3. MAURICE SACHS (d. 1944)

Eighteen-year-old Maurice Sachs served for a time as Jean Cocteau's secretary and errand boy. Sachs was dark-haired, disarming, and precociously talented with words. He wrote several novels and memoirs of life in Paris, many of which were published posthumously. Unfortunately, he was also self-destructive and untrustworthy with money. Living in Paris as a protege of Cocteau, he misused the funds Coco Chanel gave him to assemble a library for her; he sold several valuable letters and documents from Cocteau's apartment and pocketed the money for himself; and when he decided to join a seminary and become a priest (he was a convert from Judaism to Catholicism), his fellow seminarians soon had to fend off his numerous creditors who were banging at the seminary door demanding money. Sachs's vocation as a priest quickly crumbled when he fell in love with a teenaged American boy vacationing on the Mediterranean; likewise, Sachs's marriage of convenience to an American woman crumbled several years later when he fell in love with a man in the U.S. and fled back to France with him.

Despite all of these embarrassments, there must have been something intensely likable about him: his friends, including Cocteau, forgave him time and again. As a homosexual of Jewish extraction, however, Sachs was in grave danger during the German occupation of France. At first, he became romantically involved with a Nazi officer in Paris; the two of them lived together for a time. When the relationship soured, Sachs resorted to dealing in the black market in order to survive. Not long afterward, he became entangled in a web of Gestapo intrigue and began working for the Nazis as an informer. He soon proved unreliable, however, and was finally condemned to a German prison. With the approach of the Allied forces, the prison was hastily evacuated, and the prisoners were sent on a grueling forced march across Germany. Anyone who stumbled or fell was shot in the back of the head. Sachs was one of those who did not make it.

4. MAX JACOB (d. 1944)

One of the most richly creative French poets of the early twentieth century, Jacob numbered Cocteau, Picasso, and Natalie Barney among his numerous friends. Remembered as a gentle, charming, and considerate man, he was a regular contributor to Apollinaire's magazine *Les Soirees de Paris,* and was a devoted mentor to numerous young proteges. It was he who "discovered" the sixteen-year-old *enfant terrible* Raymond Radiguet and introduced him to Cocteau. Born a Jew, Jacob converted to Christianity in 1909, and became a Catholic in 1915. In 1924, he retired from city life to the Benedictine abbey of St. Benoit-sur-Loire, where he lived, on and off, in seclusion for the next twenty years; he said he could not live in Paris without succumbing regularly to sexual temptation. He fervently desired to be a devout Catholic, partly because he had a terrible fear of suffering in hell. The cruel irony is that hell on earth was already at his doorstep, and in February 1944, when he was sixty-eight years old, he was abruptly arrested by the Gestapo. His brother, sister, and brother-in-law — all Jewish — had already perished in the death camps.

Jacob's commitment to Catholicism could not save him: he was a homosexual and of Jewish extraction. Shortly after his arrest, he managed to get a short note to Cocteau telling of his fate. "I embrace you," were his final words. Cocteau and others signed a petition to obtain his release, but without result. Jacob contracted pneumonia shortly after his internment in the concentration camp at Drancy, just outside of Paris. The Nazis refused him adequate medical treatment, and he perished.

NOTE: In 1935, Adolf Hitler ordered a revision of German Paragraph 175, which already made sodomy a crime, to include proscriptions against homosexual kissing, embracing, and even homosexual fantasies. Later, Hitler's government went one step further and ordered the compulsory sterilization of homosexuals, along with epileptics, schizophrenics, the mentally retarded, and other "undesirables." In 1936, Heinrich Himmler, Hitler's second-in-command, announced that, "Homosexuals must be eliminated. Homosexuals must be eliminated root and branch." Gay men were forced to wear pink triangles on their clothing to distinguish them from other civilians, and were herded off by the tens of thousands to concentration camps, where they were tortured, worked to death, and brutally murdered. Thousands — perhaps tens of thousands — of pink triangle prisoners were executed by the Nazis. After liberation, in 1945, financial reparation, which was extended to other victims of the camps, was denied to gay victims of Naziism since they were still regarded as civil criminals under German law. Worse still, many concentration camp inmates who had been sentenced by the Nazis under Paragraph 175 were left interned after liberation since the postwar government still regarded homosexuality as a punishable crime. The West German government did not see fit to revise or abolish Hitler's anti-homosexual laws until 1969.

THE THIRD REICH'S 8 METHODS TO ACHIEVE "THE DESEXUALIZATION OF CONQUERED MALES"

As part of the Third Reich's plan to reduce the population of the countries it conquered, Nazi researcher Dr. Walther Gross devised an eight-point scheme to eradicate sexual desire and potency in Frenchmen, Poles, Russians, and other conquered males:

1. Castration, irradiation, and other mechanical damage to the male sex organs;

2. Chemical damage of the reproductive and nervous systems through the administration of poisons, including alcohol, nicotine, cocaine, and morphine;

3. Bacterial damage through the deliberate introduction of various infectious diseases into conquered populations;

4. Nutritional deficiencies brought about by depriving men of vitamins — especially Vitamin E — and minerals such as calcium, magnesium, and phosphorus;

5. Subjecting conquered males to severe mental and emotional strain, in order to engender impotence;

6. Encouragement of homosexuality, masturbation, and other sexual "deviations" among inferior races, which, in line with Hitler's thinking, "severely weakened" a populace;

7. The creation of a psychological environment in which fear is pervasive;

8. The creation of conditions of prolonged exhaustion, which would have the effect of destroying all sexual appetite in the men.

SOURCE: *The Sexual History of the World War* by Dr. Magnus Hirschfeld (and eleven collaborators). New York: Cadillac Publishing Co., 1946.

6 MEN WHO WERE FULL- OR PART-TIME TRANSVESTITES

1. JENNY SAVALETTE DE LANGE

Wandering about Paris and Versailles in her dated clothes and her wide-brimmed hats, the woman known as Jenny Savalette de Lange aroused little curiosity. She was, according to her contemporaries, no beauty: she was gaunt and tall, with hard features and a sullen look. She always carried an umbrella. When she died at Versailles on May 6, 1858, her body was quietly handed over to two old women to prepare it for burial. It was then discovered that Jenny was, in fact, a man.

Apparently, for almost seventy years, no one had known her secret; she had few friends, and although from some reports she had had various lovers, she never married. She had lived most of her life on a generous government pension, although no one could figure out exactly how she had gotten the pension in the first place, or why

Gossip soon began to spread that Jenny was actually Louis XVII, the son of Marie Antoinette and King Louis XVI. Captured by French revolutionaries along with his mother and father as they tried to flee France in 1791, the ten-year-old Louis had allegedly died in prison of tuberculosis shortly after his parents were guillotined. However, his last months in prison had been veiled in secrecy, and for years afterward there were stories that the boy had actually escaped with the help of a conspiracy of monarchists who planned to restore him one day as rightful heir to the throne of France. Over the years, more than thirty people had claimed to be the young prince. In the case of Jenny Savalette de Lange, nothing could be proved and the mystery was never solved, despite the efforts of numerous people to find out exactly who she was and where she had come from. Jenny's death certificate stated simply that she was "an unknown man . . . a bachelor."

2. LORD CORNBURY

Cornbury served as colonial governor of New York and New Jersey between 1702 and 1709, and then as governor of North Carolina from 1711 to 1712. During his administrations, he became notorious as both a drunkard and a transvestite: he was called "the governor in petticoats." Dressed one night in his wife's clothes, he was detained as a drunk vagrant by his own officers, who did not recognize him at first. On other occasions, Cornbury allegedly paraded around the fort dressed in elaborate and sumptuous female attire, a distraction to all public business. He claimed that his transvestism was meant as a tribute to his cousin, Queen Anne. There is a portrait of him (currently owned by the New York Historical Society) in full drag — in a classic, unpretentious blue gown, long white gloves, and a small lace or ribbon topknot. His face was distinctly unattractive, with thick lips, carefully arched eyebrows, and double chin. Cornbury was one of the most corrupt and despised public officials of his day; his political career apparently ended in 1712, and he died in 1723 at the age of sixty-two.

3. BARBETTE

"Unforgettable." "A theatrical masterpiece." "An angel, a flower, a bird." That was how Jean Cocteau described Barbette, the female impersonator whose act at the Casino de Paris became the toast of Paris in the late 1920s. An accomplished acrobat and tightrope dancer, Barbette would first appear onstage in a sumptuous evening gown, usually of lamés and paillettes, with trimmings of feathers and lace. The evening gown was soon removed, revealing beneath it the outfit of a woman trapeze artist. Accompanied by the music of Wagner and Rimsky-Korsakov, Barbette would then mount the highwire or trapeze, and swing and dance in mid-air high above the audience's heads. The ten-minute act always ended the same way, with a touch of high drama – descending from the trapeze and moving towards the audience, Barbette would dramatically remove his wig and reveal that he was a man. The routine became almost legendary in various European capitals – among them Berlin, Warsaw, Madrid, and Copenhagen – and he was admired not only by Cocteau but by Igor Stravinsky and numerous other composers, artists, and writers of the day.

Barbette's background seemed slightly incongruous for the glamour of the Casino de Paris. Born Vander Clyde, in a small town in Texas in 1904, he got his start as a trapeze artist in San Antonio, before he began to develop his own solo act disguised as a woman. After performing across the United States, he signed with the William Morris Agency and was sent to England and Paris in the fall of 1923, where his performances were received as a theatrical tour de force. "I myself have seen no comparable display of artistry on the stage since Nijinsky," Cocteau wrote a friend. After more than a decade of popular acclaim, Barbette's spectacular career ended abruptly when he became ill with a sudden crippling affliction of the bones and joints. He returned to Texas, where he became an acrobatic trainer. Barbette can be seen, briefly, as a lady in a theater box in Jean Cocteau's 1930 film *Blood of a Poet.* His theatrical career provided part of the inspiration for Blake Edward's 1982 musical comedy *Victor/Victoria.*

4. STELLA WALSH

An Olympic gold medalist in track-and-field, Stella Walsh was considered one of the most formidable woman runners of the 1930s. During the 1932 and 1936 Olympics, she won a total of five gold medals, along with three silver and one bronze. Later, she got married, and retired to a suburb of Cleveland, where she dedicated herself to working with children in athletics. To the people who knew her, it came as a shock when, in 1981, she was robbed and shot to death in a department store parking lot. It came as an even greater shock to the sports world when, during preparations for the funeral, it was discovered that Stella Walsh was a man.

Born Stanislawa Walaslewicz in Poland in 1911, Walsh had often aroused comment during competition in the 1930s for her extraordinary musculature and excessive body hair; it was often remarked that she ran like a man. In 1956, having retired from competition, Walsh married Harry Olson in Las Vegas; they separated after eight weeks, but never divorced. After Walsh's death, Olson said he was surprised by the report of his wife's true sex. He told the press that he and Walsh had had sex only "a couple of times, and she wouldn't let me have any lights on." Despite the revelation that Walsh was a man, the U.S. Olympic Committee announced there would be no attempt to posthumously retract Walsh's Olympic medals.

5. ALEXANDER WOOLLCOTT

The acerbic theater critic and unctuous radio sage of the twenties, thirties, and early forties was a pampered child whose sisters incessantly dressed him as a girl. He founded his college's first dramatic club but demanded that he play all of the feminine leads in its productions. After that, he started appearing at parties dressed in women's clothes and often handed out calling cards that read, "Alexandra Woollcott." Secretly, he was tormented by his confused sexual feelings. His torment was aggravated by the taunts of his classmates. "I wonder if he has to sit down to pee," said one. Others called him "freak" or "sissy." By his sophomore year, Woollcott seriously considered suicide.

The torment and confusion lasted well into his adult life. After he achieved fame as a journalist and a theater critic, he invited playwright Anita Loos to his home one afternoon and showed her a picture of himself dressed as a woman in college. He confessed, with tears in his eyes, that he had always wanted to be a girl. "All my life I've wanted to be a mother," he added sorrowfully. Described by Edna Ferber as "that New Jersey Nero who thinks his pinafore is a toga," Woollcott later made a profitable hobby of designing women's clothing. At home, he often appeared to guests dressed in vast, flowing dressing gowns with huge, wide-brimmed hats. By then, he was hideously overweight, and in these bizarre get-ups, he often looked, according to friend Harpo Marx, "like something that had gotten loose from Macy's Thanksgiving Day parade."

6. MAGNUS HIRSCHFELD

Once described as "the Einstein of sex," Hirschfeld was a short, pudgy, effeminate neurologist who, in late nineteenth century Germany, became a leading pioneer in the fledgling field of sexual research. Independently wealthy, he was free to devote himself to writing, education, and working for legal reforms. In 1897, he founded one of the first organizations to defend homosexuals' rights, the Scientific Humanitarian Committee, which was devoted to repealing harsh anti-gay laws in the German penal code. In 1919, he founded the world's first sex research institute, the Institute of Sexual Science in Berlin, which was a repository for books, magazines, pictures, personal testimonies, and other scientific material dealing with sex.

Because of his research, and because he was Jewish, Hirschfeld was reviled by the Nazis; in 1933, they ransacked his Institute and burned much of its priceless collection of over 20,000 volumes and 35,000 pictures. Hirschfeld himself was once severely beaten and left for dead by a group of Nazis on a street in Munich. He was forced to flee the country, and died in France in 1935. Hirschfeld was himself both gay and a transvestite. In fact, he coined the word "transvestism." "Beneath the duality of sex there is a oneness," he once wrote. "Every male is potentially a female and every female potentially a male. If a man wants to understand a woman, he must discover the woman in himself, and if a woman would understand a man, she must dig in her own consciousness to discover her own masculine traits "

14 GAY OR BISEXUAL FATHERS

1. ALEXANDER THE GREAT (356-323 B.C.), Macedonian ruler

Alexander had one son, the result of his marriage to an Asian princess. In the power struggle and bloodbath that followed Alexander's death, the boy, who was only thirteen, was murdered.

2. EDWARD II (1284-1327), king of England

Despite his almost exclusively homosexual nature, Edward dutifully produced a male heir by his queen, Isabella. In 1327, Edward was deposed and brutally murdered by Isabella and her lover, Roger Mortimer. Edward's son, then only fifteen, became king of England — a puppet king until, just three years later, he asserted his independence, had Mortimer executed, and sent his scheming mother into retirement.

3. IL SODOMA (1477-1549), Italian painter

His name says it all: the High Renaissance painter gained a wide reputation during his lifetime as a homosexual. But Il Sodoma still found the energy to father a daughter, Faustina. Faustina married one of her father's former boyfriends.

4. JAMES I (1566-1625), king of England

Knowledge of James's homosexuality was so widespread that when he succeeded Elizabeth I as monarch of England, people shouted in the streets, "Elizabeth was King, now James is Queen!" In his lifetime, James produced a daughter and two male heirs. His younger son ascended to the throne as Charles I in 1625. James was himself the son of a homosexual father, the notorious profligate Lord Darnley, second husband of Mary, Queen of Scots.

5. WALT WHITMAN (1819-1892), U.S. poet

Whitman claimed to have fathered at least six illegitimate children, and wove rather fantastic and sometimes inconsistent stories about them. Some historians dismiss the claim as defensive bravado, Whitman's anxious answer to those who tried to label

Were Walt Whitman's claims of having fathered six illegitimate children true, or just defensive bravado?

Courtesy Library of Congress, Brady-Handy Collection

him homosexual. Others are not quite so sure, although no trace of the children has ever been discovered.

6. JOHN ADDINGTON SYMONDS (1840-1893), English essayist and historian

In spite of his lifelong obsession with homosexuality and his dalliances with gondoliers, college boys, and the like, Symonds remained married for twenty-eight years. "Our domestic relations are not of the happiest," he discreetly wrote a friend, "and we get along best when we are away from one another." Symonds had four daughters. When Symonds' unpublished, explicitly homoerotic memoirs were sealed in the London Library after his death, his youngest daughter, Katharine, was the first person to ask permission to read them.

7. PAUL VERLAINE (1844-1896), French poet

Verlaine had one son, Georges, whom he abused as an infant and neglected as a young adult. An alcoholic, Georges led a pathetic, listless life, before dying of drink in 1926 at the age of fifty-four.

8. OSCAR WILDE (1854-1900), Irish playwright and wit

Wilde married when he was twenty-nine, and had two sons, Cyril and Vyvyan. After Wilde was sentenced in 1895 to two years hard labor for having committed homosexual acts, his wife took the boys, then aged eight and nine, to Switzerland and changed the family name. "That the law should decide and take upon itself that I am unfit to be with my own children is something quite horrible to me," Wilde wrote in *De Profundis*. "The disgrace of prison is as nothing compared to it." After his release, Wilde petitioned his wife, unsuccessfully, for permission to see the boys, but she would only send him photographs of them. "I want my boys," he wrote in anguish to a friend. As it turned out, Wilde saw neither his wife nor his sons ever again. He died in exile in Paris in 1900. The younger son, Vyvyan, later wrote several favorable books about his father, including *Son of Oscar Wilde* and *A Pictorial Biography of Oscar Wilde.*

9. ANDRE GIDE (1869-1951), French author

Gide was fifty-four when he fathered an illegitimate daughter, Catherine; the mother was Elisabeth van Bysselberghe, a well-known feminist. Gide lived to be eighty-two, long enough to see himself a grandfather.

10. LORD ALFRED DOUGLAS (1870-1945), English poet

After his fateful friendship with Oscar Wilde ended in scandal, Douglas renounced homosexuality and became a fervent convert to the Roman Catholic church. Two years after Wilde's death, Douglas married Olive Custance, a minor poetess, and they had one son, Raymond. Olive's father, Colonel Custance, took a dim view of Douglas as both a husband and a parent. Alleging that Douglas was a cruel and irresponsible father — and certainly on the basis of Douglas' notorious relationship with Wilde — the Colonel successfully sued to have young Raymond taken taken away from his parents. The Colonel's action tore Douglas' marriage apart, as poor Olive sided first with her father, then with her husband, then with her father again. Douglas' marriage ended in a shambles, and his attempts to win back custody of his son were unsuccessful. The custody battles and family rifts took their toll on little Raymond: he grew up with severe emotional problems. At the age of twenty-five, he was diagnosed as schizophrenic and was committed to a private mental hospital. He spent much of his life in and out of such institutions, and died in one in 1964.

11. W. SOMERSET MAUGHAM (1874-1965), English author

Maugham once said of himself, "I tried to persuade myself that I was three-quarters normal and that only a quarter of me was queer — whereas really it was the other way around." In 1915, Maugham fathered an illegitimate daughter, Elizabeth; two years later, he married the girl's mother. The marriage was a tragic, bitter mistake. Maugham angrily told his wife: "I married you because I thought it the best thing for your happiness and for Elizabeth's welfare, but I did not marry you because I loved you, and you were only too aware of that." They were divorced in 1929, and young Elizabeth grew up to despise her famous father. When Maugham was eighty-eight, Elizabeth tried to have him put away on the grounds that he was senile and incompetent. Maugham retaliated by legally disowning her and adopting his lover, Alan Searle, as his son. In court, Elizabeth had the adoption nullified and had herself restored as Maugham's legal heir.

12. VASLAV NIJINSKY (1890-1950), Russian dancer

Isadora Duncan once suggested to Nijinsky that he father her next child; he said no. For one thing, he was already involved in a sexual relationship, an intense and possessive one, with dance impressario Serge Diaghilev. However, in 1913, Nijinsky abruptly turned his back on Diaghilev — on homosexuality in general — and impulsively married the daughter of a Hungarian actress during a dance tour in South America. They remained married until Nijinsky's death thirty-seven years later, and had two daughters. In 1980, when Herbert Ross's film biography *Nijinsky* first opened, one of Nijinsky's daughters, Kyra, then in her sixties, condemned it. She was particularly annoyed at the film's emphasis on her father's love affair with Diaghilev. "I certainly am not the child of my father and Diaghilev!" she indignantly reminded the press.

13. LEONARD BERNSTEIN (b. 1918), U.S. conductor and composer

Although he was, in the words of his biographer Joan Peyser, "rampantly homosexual" for the early part of his life, Bernstein married in 1951 when he was in his early thirties. He and his wife

Felicia had three children: two girls and a boy. According to a 1987 interview with Peyser, "More recently [Bernstein] has again been promiscuously homosexual..."

14. YUKIO MISHIMA (1925-1970), Japanese author
Mishima had two children, both of whom are still living.

7 WELL-KNOWN WOMEN WHO MARRIED GAY OR BISEXUAL MEN

1. MARY, QUEEN OF SCOTS (1542-1587)
Her second husband was the strikingly handsome Lord Darnley, a cousin. She was twenty-three; he was only twenty. Although she married him for love, it was a tragic choice: Darnley, though muscular and exceptionally good looking, was emotionally weak and vicious, and although he provided her with an heir — the future James I of England — he apparently preferred sodomizing his young grooms and stableboys. Within months, Mary's love withered into contempt, and barely two years after they were married, Darnley was strangled to death, most likely by a conspiracy of nobles; he was allegedly having sex with one of his pages at the time.

2. LILLIAN RUSSELL (1861-1922), U.S. singer and actress
She was married four times. Her third marriage was to gay tenor Giovanni Perugini. Friends described the union as "a marriage of convenience — his." It didn't last long. She resented his nagging, his violent outbursts, and his insults. The marriage ended after less than two months, after he tried to throw her from a seventh-story window. Defending the action, Perugini told a reporter, "Do you realize the enormity of this woman's offense — her crime? Do you know what she did to me? Why, sir, she took all the pillows; she used my rouge; she misplaced my manicure set; she used my special handkerchief perfume for her bath ... Once she threatened to spank me, and she did, with a hairbrush, too. You can't expect a fellow to take a spanking with equanimity, can you?"

Husband and wife Charles Laughton and Elsa Lanchester starred together in more than half a dozen films, including *Rembrandt* (1936).

3. RUTH ST. DENIS (1878-1968), U.S. dancer

Her husband was dancer Ted Shawn, renowned as "the father of American dance," with whom she founded Denishawn, the innovative American school and dance company that produced such illustrious pupils as Martha Graham. Although they remained married for over fifty years, they separated after seventeen, after they both fell in love with the same young man. Shawn blamed the sudden, overwhelming onset of his homosexuality on her numerous infidelities.

4. ELSA LANCHESTER (1902-1986), English actress

Her husband, actor Charles Laughton, revealed his homosexuality to her two years after they were married. She went deaf for a week after he made the announcement. However, she soon recovered, and they remained married for thirty-three years — no longer lovers, but still close friends and companions — until Laughton's death of bone cancer in 1962. They starred together in more than half a dozen films, including *Rembrandt, The Private Life of Henry VIII,* and *Witness for the Prosecution.*

5. VERA PANOVA (1905-1973), Soviet writer

As an officially esteemed novelist and playwright in the Soviet Union, she extended whatever protection she could to her many gay friends and associates, including her own husband, writer David Dar, who publicly revealed his homosexuality after he had emigrated to Israel in 1977.

6. ANNABELLA (b. 1909), French actress

She married actor Tyrone Power in 1939. They were divorced in 1948.

7. CARSON McCULLERS (1917-1967), U.S. writer

She married Reeves McCullers in 1937, when she was nineteen, divorced him five years later in 1942, and then remarried him in 1945. The marriage disintegrated the first time when they both fell in love with the same man, composer David Diamond. After their remarriage, Reeves became increasingly tormented, not only by his homosexual feelings, but by feelings of living in his wife's shadow. He began contemplating suicide, and decided to take her with him. When he was driving her to the doctor's one day, she noticed two lengths of coiled rope on the floorboard. "We're going out into the forest," he told her, "and hang ourselves. But first, we'll stop and buy a bottle of brandy. We'll drink it for old times' sake." When he stopped at a liquor store, she fled the car. She never saw him again. Two months later, he committed suicide with an overdose of barbiturates.

OSCAR WILDE'S 3 WOMEN HE WOULD HAVE MARRIED "WITH PLEASURE"

1. QUEEN VICTORIA

2. SARAH BERNHARDT

3. LILLIE LANGTRY

In 1899, the year before his death, Wilde told a friend, "The three women I have most admired are Queen Victoria, Sarah Bernhardt, and Lillie Langtry. I would have married any one of them with pleasure. The first had great dignity, the second a lovely voice, the third a perfect figure."

9 GAY MEN WHO DIDN'T LET ADVANCING AGE STOP THEM

1. ALEXANDER VON HUMBOLDT (1769-1859), German explorer and scientist

At the age of sixty, he was exploring uncharted, remote areas of Russia, Siberia, and Central Asia. The last 25 years of his life, beginning when he was 65, were devoted to writing *Kosmos,* a four-volume scientific compendium for the general public. He was actively at work on a fifth volume to the series when he died suddenly, at the age of ninety.

2. GEORGE CUKOR (1899-1983), U.S. film director

Cukor was 73 when he directed the motion picture *Travels With My Aunt,* 76 when he directed *The Blue Bird,* and 79 when he directed the critically acclaimed made-for-TV movie *The Corn Is Green,* with Katharine Hepburn. He directed his last film, *Rich and Famous,* when he was 81.

George Santayana: philosopher, novelist, poet, and educator. He wrote: "There is no cure for birth and death save to enjoy the interval."

3. MICHELANGELO (1475-1564), Italian sculptor and painter

He completed the tomb of Julius II when he was seventy. Six days before his death, at the age of 88, he was still at work sculpting the *Rondanini Pieta.*

4. EDWARD EVERETT HORTON (1886-1970), U.S. actor

A veteran of over eighty films beginning in the early 1920s, Horton continued to work throughout his seventies and into his eighties. His last film, *Cold Turkey,* was made in 1970, when the actor was 84.

5. CAMILLE SAINT-SAENS (1835-1921), French composer

When he was 80, he was sent by the French government to the Panama-Pacific Exposition, where he was guest conductor of a series of concerts. At 86, he was still touring to perform his works.

6. GEORGE SANTAYANA (1863-1952), Spanish-U.S. philosopher

When Santayana was in his early eighties, he was immersed in the writing of *Dominations and Powers,* an analysis of man in society. At the age of 88, he began work on a translation of Lorenzo de Medici's love poem "Ambra."

7. E.M. FORSTER (1879-1970), English writer

Forster was in his seventies when he wrote, with Eric Crozier, the libretto for Benjamin Britten's opera *Billy Budd.* At the age of 80, he was still reviewing books for the *Spectator* and the *Observer.* At 81, he appeared as a witness in the impassioned obscenity trial of D.H. Lawrence's *Lady Chatterley's Lover.*

8. EDWARD CARPENTER (1844-1929), English writer and reformer

At 71, Carpenter wrote *The Healing of Nations,* a denunciation of war. At 73, he wrote *Three Ballads,* a collection of satirical pieces. At 74, he edited *Poems Written During the Great War 1914–1918,* and translated many of the poems included.

9. ANDRE GIDE (1869-1951), French writer

He was in his mid-seventies when he wrote "Theseus," his last great literary work. At the age of 78, Gide won the Nobel Prize for literature. At the age of 81, he published the final volume of his *Journal.*

6 INSTANCES OF GAY LOVERS BURIED TOGETHER

1. ROBERT DE MONTESQUIOI and GABRIEL D'YTURRI

For twenty years, Gabriel d'Yturri was secretary and lover to French poet Robert de Montesquioi, the model for Baron de Charlus in Proust's *Remembrance of Things Past.* Yturri died in 1905 of complications from diabetes. His last words to Montesquioi, before lapsing into a coma, were, "Thank you for teaching me to understand all these beautiful things." Sixteen years later, Montesquioi died of kidney disease. In accordance with his instructions, he was buried beside Yturri in a cemetery at Versailles.

2. ROBERT ROSS and OSCAR WILDE

Wilde died in Paris in 1900, and his remains were temporarily buried in a small cemetery at Bagneux, before being moved nine years later to a permanent tomb at Pere Lachaise Cemetery in Paris. In 1950, during a ceremony commemorating the fiftieth anniversary of Wilde's death, the tomb was opened and the ashes of Wilde's longtime friend and literary executor, Robert Ross, were placed inside. Ross had died in 1918; he had often claimed that he was "the first boy Oscar ever had."

3. CROCE-SPINELLI and SIVEL

Croce-Spinelli and Sivel were two nineteenth-century balloonists who died together in a ballooning accident 26,000 feet over India in 1875; they were asphyxiated when the air grew too thin. The huge marble monument over the tomb they share in Pere Lachaise Cemetery portrays the men lying together, side-by-side, hand-in-hand, presumably naked but covered by a sculpted sheet from the waist down. There are flowers in their hands. The tomb, one of the most talked-about monuments in Pere Lachaise, has been called a "tribute to their comradeship in life and death."

4. CONRADIN OF SICILY and FREDERICK OF BADEN

Sixteen-year-old Conradin of Sicily was the last of the Hohenstaufen kings. Betrayed in his attempts to hold onto his crown, the adolescent king was beheaded by political enemies in 1268. His 21-year-old lover and advisor, Frederick of Baden, voluntarily joined him on the scaffold. The two lovers were interred together in the church of the monastery of Santa Maria del Carmine in Naples. For centuries after, the burial place was a shrine for gay lovers, and in 1847, the Crown Prince of Bavaria commissioned a marble statue to be erected there in Conradin's memory.

5. EPAMINONDAS and TWO YOUNG SOLDIERS

After being killed in the battle of Mantinea, the Theban general Epaminondas (418-362 B.C.) was buried in a tomb with two young soldiers who had been his lovers and who had also fallen in battle.

6. BENJAMIN BRITTEN and PETER PEARS

British composer Benjamin Britten died in 1976. Tenor Peter Pears, Britten's lover and collaborator for over forty years, died ten years later, of a heart attack. Pears was laid to rest next to Britten in a grave in Aldeburgh, England.

26 PARTING THOUGHTS

1. GORE VIDAL, U.S. writer

"There is no such thing as a homosexual, no such thing as a heterosexual. Everyone has homosexual and heterosexual desires and impulses and responses . . . But trust a nitwit society like this one to think that there are only two categories — fag and straight — and if you're the first, you want to be a woman, and if you're the second, you're a pretty damned wonderful guy . . . Very few so-called fags are feminine in their ways and very few heteros can be regarded as wonderful."

2. GLENN SWANN, U.S. porno star

"I'm a very sexual person and I prefer to describe myself as just being sexual. Not gay, not heterosexual, and not bisexual. Just sexual."

3. JOHN ADDINGTON SYMONDS, English essayist and historian

"We maintain that we have the right to exist after the fashion which nature made us. And if we cannot alter your laws, we shall go on breaking them. You may condemn us to infamy, exile, prison — as you formerly burned witches. You may degrade our emotional instincts and drive us into vice and misery. But you will not eradicate inverted sexuality."

4. ARISTIPPUS, Greek philosopher

"The art of life lies in taking pleasures as they pass, and the keenest pleasures aren't intellectual, nor are they always moral."

5. PAT CALIFIA, U.S. writer

"It's a much more honorable act to rim a total stranger than it is to deny a poor woman an abortion, and it's more righteous to help an underage lesbian sneak into the bar than it is to force her to pray in school."

6. QUENTIN CRISP, English writer

"There are many aspects of the contemporary gay subculture that I find ridiculous, but nothing could be more ridiculous than to say, as some critics have, that I am antihomosexual simply because I do not embrace every twitty gay fad that comes along. I think that a lifetime of listening to disco music is a high price to pay for one's sexual preference."

7. NED ROREM, U.S. composer
"Homosexuality, unlike negritude or womanhood, is a part-time job."

8. HARVEY FIERSTEIN, U.S. playwright and actor
"Gay liberation should not be a license to be a perpetual adolescent. If you deny yourself commitment, then what can you do with your life?"

9. CHRISTOPHER ISHERWOOD, British-U.S. writer
"It seems to me that the real clue to your sex-orientation lies in your romantic feelings rather than in your sexual feelings. If you are really gay, you are able to fall in love with a man, not just enjoy having sex with him."

10. D.H. LAWRENCE, British writer
"I believe the nearest I have come to perfect love was with a young coal miner when I was about sixteen."

11. E.M. FORSTER, English writer
"I want to love a strong young man of the lower classes and be loved by him, and even hurt by him."

12. RANDY SHILTS, U.S. writer
"I could not imagine writing a biography of anybody without discussing his sex life. I don't think you can fully understand anybody unless you understand how they do or do not integrate their sexuality into who they are as a human being."

13. ROBERT MORLEY, English actor
"It's a wonder you have any homosexuals in America, because daily, the children are bombarded with anti-homosexual propaganda. You even pronounce the word differently than we do — you give it a rather nasty sound."

14. JERRY FALWELL, U.S. politician
"There's a lot of talk these days about homosexuals coming

out of the closet. I didn't know they'd been in the closet. I do know they've always been in the gutter."

15. OSCAR WILDE, British playwright and wit
"We are all in the gutter, but some of us are looking at the stars."

16. GEORGE LINCOLN ROCKWELL, U.S. Nazi party leader
"I'd also purge the queers. I despise them worst of all. They're one of the ugliest problems of our society, and they must be removed — I don't know if with gas, or what . . . They're the ultimate symbol of a decaying civilization."

17. P. THOMAS CARY, former San Francisco police officer
"While we were watching a training film of the Dan White riot at city hall, officers threw things at the TV screen and shouted 'Kill the faggots!'"

18. ANITA BRYANT, U.S. entertainer
"There was one point where our daughters, Gloria and Barbara, told me that they didn't want to hold hands with their little girlfriends anymore. They were afraid people would think they were homosexuals."

19. HARVEY MILK, U.S. gay activist
"The fact is that more people have been slaughtered in the name of religion than for any other single reason. That, that my friends, that is true perversion!"

20. LILLIAN CARTER, mother of President Jimmy Carter
"I don't know a gay from a hole in the ground — in my part of the country, we don't have 'em."

21. DR. EVELYN HOOKER, U.S. scientist
"Are homosexuals social outcasts? My God. Christopher Isherwood, Howard Brown, Merle Miller, Sidney Abbott, John Maynard Keynes. Are these people social outcasts? . . . Some of the most moral men I know are homosexuals."

22. FRANK ZAPPA, U.S. musician
"My attitude toward anybody's sexual persuasion is this: without deviation from the norm, progress is not possible."

23. PETTE MIDLER, U.S. entertainer

"For Christ's sake, open your mouths; don't you people get tired of being stepped on?"

24. PAUL NEWMAN, U.S. actor

"I'm a supporter of gay rights. And not a closet supporter, either. From the time I was a kid, I have never been able to understand attacks upon the gay community. There are so many qualities that make up a human being . . . by the time I get through with all the things that I really admire about people, what they do with their private parts is probably so low on the list that it is irrelevant."

25. VALERIE PERRINE, U.S. actress

"Most of my male friends are gay, and that seems perfectly natural to me. I mean, who wouldn't like cock?"

26. ADDAEUS, Macedonian philosopher

"When you meet a boy who pleases you, take action at once. Don't be polite – just grab him by the balls and strike while the iron is hot."

INDEX

A wide variety of books with gay and lesbian themes are available from Alyson Publications. For a catalog, or to be placed on our mailing list, please write to: